STUDY GUIDE

KENRICK S. THOMPSON

SOCIETY: THE BASICS

EIGHTH EDITION

JOHN J. MACIONIS

PEARSON
Prentice
Hall

Upper Saddle River, New Jersey 07458

© 2006 by PEARSON EDUCATION, INC.
Upper Saddle River, New Jersey 07458

10 9 8 7 6 5 4 3 2

ISBN 0-13-154616-3

Printed in the United States of America

Table of Contents

Preface

This study guide has been written to enhance the foundation of sociological ideas and issues that are presented in the text *Society, 8/e,* by John Macionis. To help you review and think about the material found in the text, the study guide has been organized into several different sections to accompany each chapter in the text.

- Part I provides a ***Chapter Outline*** allowing you to organize segments of information from each chapter in the text.
- Part II on ***Learning Objectives*** identifies the basic knowledge, explanations, comparisons, and understandings you should have after reading and reflecting on each chapter.
- Part III is entitled ***Key Concepts*** and has the important concepts the chapter defined. You are asked to write the appropriate concept in the blank space found in each definition.
- Part IV, ***Important Researchers,*** cites many of the researchers found in the text, with space provided for you to write out important ideas, findings, etc.
- Part V provides ***Study Questions***, including true-false, multiple choice, matching, fill-in, and discussion questions.
- Part VI, ***Answers to Study Questions***, includes a list of the page numbers where the answers to these questions can be found.
- Part VII, ***In Focus--Important Issues***, gives you an opportunity to answer questions relating to some of the more important concepts and ideas presented in each chapter.

Comments and suggestions may be directed to me at the following address:

kthompson@asumh.edu

KST

<table>
<tr><td>Chapter
1</td><td></td></tr>
</table>

Chapter 1

Sociology: Perspective, Theory, and Method

PART I: CHAPTER OUTLINE

I.   The Sociological Perspective
   A.   Seeing the General in the Particular
   B.   Seeing the Strange in the Familiar
   C.   Seeing Individuality in Social Context
   D.   Benefits of the Sociological Perspective
   E.   Applied Sociology
   F.   The Importance of a Global Perspective

II.   The Origins of Sociology
   A.   Social Change and Sociology
      1.   Industrial Technology
      2.   The Growth of Cities
      3.   Political Change
   B.   Science and Sociology
   C.   Gender and Race: Marginal Voices

III.   Sociological Theory
   A.   The Structural-Functional Approach
   B.   The Social-Conflict Approach
   C.   The Symbolic-Interaction Approach

IV.   Three Ways to Do Sociology
   A.   Scientific Sociology
      1.   Concepts, Variables, and Measurement
      2.   Reliability and Validity
      3.   Correlation and Cause
      4.   The Ideal of Objectivity
   B.   Interpretive Sociology
      1.   The Importance of Meaning
      2.   Weber's Concept of *Verstehen*
   C.   Critical Sociology
      1.   The Importance of Change
      2.   Sociology as Politics
   D.   Methods and Theory

V.   Research Ethics
   A.   Gender and Research

VI.   Research Methods
   A.   Testing a Hypothesis: The Experiment
      1.   An Illustration: The "Stanford County Prison" Experiment

PART II: LEARNING OBJECTIVES

- To define sociology and understand the basic components of the sociological perspective.
- To provide examples of the ways in which social forces affect our everyday lives.
- To recognize the importance of taking a global perspective in order to appreciate the interdependence of our world's nations and people.
- To recognize the benefits of using the sociological perspective.
- To be familiar with the origins of sociology.
- To identify and discuss the differences among the three major theoretical approaches used by sociologists in the analysis of society.
- To be familiar with the three ways to do sociology.
- To understand scientific and interpretive sociology.
- To review the fundamental requirements for engaging in scientific investigation using the sociological perspective.
- To appreciate the importance of research ethics.
- To be familiar with the major research methods in sociology and how to use available data.

PART III: KEY CONCEPTS

1. _____ is the systematic study of human society.
2. Studying the larger world and our society's place in it refers to taking a _____ _____.
3. _____ *countries* are the richest nations with the highest overall standards of living.
4. The world's _____ *countries* are nations with a standard of living about average for the world as a whole.
5. About one half the world's population live in the sixty _____ *countries*, nations with a low standard of living.
6. A way of understanding based on science is known as _____.
7. A _____ is a statement of how and why specific facts are related.
8. A _____ _____ is a basic image of society that guides thinking and research.

9. The _____ approach is a framework for building theory that sees society as a complex system whose parts work together to promote solidarity and stability.

10. The term _____ _____ refers to any relatively stable pattern of social behavior.

11. The consequences of any social pattern for the operation of society refer to _____ _____.

12. _____ _____ are the recognized and intended consequences of any social pattern.

13. _____ _____ are consequences that are largely unrecognized and unintended.

14. The undesirable consequences of any social pattern for the operation of society refer to _____ _____.

15. The _____ approach is a framework for building theory that sees society as an arena of inequality that generates conflict and change.

16. A _____ *orientation* refers to a concern with broad patterns that shape society as a whole.

17. A _____ *orientation* refers to a close-up focus on social interaction in specific situations.

18. The _____ approach is a framework for building theory that sees society as the product of the everyday interactions of individuals.

19. _____ is a logical system that bases knowledge on direct, systematic observation.

20. A _____ is a mental construct that represents some part of the world in a simplified form.

21. _____ are concepts whose values change from case to case.

22. A procedure for determining the value of a variable in a specific case is known as _____.

23. _____ refers to consistency in measurement.

24. _____ refers to precision in measuring exactly what one intends to measure.

25. A _____ refers to a relationship by which two (or more) variables change together.

26. A relationship in which change in one variable (the independent variable) causes change in another (the dependent variable) is known as _____ _____ _____.

27. _____ _____ is the study that focuses on the meanings people attach to their social world.

28. _____ _____ is the study of society that focuses on the needs for social change.

29. In recent years sociologists have become aware of the fact that research is affected by _____, the personal traits and social positions that members of a society attach to being female or male.

30. A _____ _____ is a systematic plan for conducting research.

31. A research method for investigating cause and effect under controlled conditions refers to an _____.

32. A research method in which subjects respond to a series of statements or questions in a questionnaire or an interview is called a _____.

33. _____ _____ is a research method by which investigators systematically observe people while joining them in their routine activities.

34. _____ refers to exaggerated descriptions applied to every person in some category.

PART IV: IMPORTANT RESEARCHERS

In the space provided below each of the following researchers, write two or three sentences to help you remember his or her respective contributions to sociology.

Jane Addams   Herbert Spencer

Emile Durkheim   Karl Marx

Max Weber   Robert Merton

Peter Berger   C. Wright Mills

Lenore Weitzman   W.E.B. Du Bois

Harriet Martineau   Auguste Comte

PART V: STUDY QUESTIONS

True-False

1.	T	F	When it comes to love and most other dimensions of our lives, the decisions we make result from what philosophers call "free will."
2.	T	F	The *middle-income countries* of the world are primarily found in Latin America, Eastern Europe, and much of southern Africa.
3.	T	F	A *New Industrial economy, the growth of cities,* and *new ideas about democracy and political freedom*s are identified as factors that helped people to view the world sociologically.
4.	T	F	A *theory* is a statement of how and why specific facts are related.
5.	T	F	*Latent functions* refer to social processes that appear on the surface to be functional for society, but in actuality are detrimental.
6.	T	F	The *symbolic-interactionist* approach presents society less in terms of abstract generalizations and more as everyday experiences.

7.   T   F   Max Weber said that people doing scientific research must strive to be *value-free*.

8.   T   F   *Androcentricity* refers to approaching an issue from a male perspective.

Multiple Choice

1.   What is the *essential wisdom* of sociology?

    (a)   Patterns in life are predestined.
    (b)   Society is essentially nonpatterned.
    (c)   Surrounding society affects our actions, thoughts, and feelings.
    (d)   Common sense needs to guide sociological investigations.

2.   The sociological perspective involves *seeing the strange in the familiar*. Which of the following best provides the essential meaning of this phrase?

    (a)   Sociology interprets social life primarily relying on common sense.
    (b)   Sociologists believe intuition rather than logic is the preferred way to study society.
    (c)   Sociologists focus on the bizarre behaviors that occur in society.
    (d)   Sociologists work to avoid the assumption that human behavior is simply a matter of what people decide to do.

3.   Which sociologist, in a systematic empirical study, linked the incidence of *suicide* to the degree of *social integration* of different categories of people?

    (a)   Emile Durkheim
    (b)   Max Weber
    (c)   Robert Merton
    (d)   C. Wright Mills

4.   *Low-income countries* are described as nations with

    (a)   a low standard of living.
    (b)   limited natural resources and large populations.
    (c)   per capita incomes of less than $15,000.
    (d)   no industrialization and limited natural resources.

5.   Which of the following is *not* identified as a reason a *global perspective* is so important?

    (a)   Societies the world over are increasingly interconnected.
    (b)   Many problems that we face in the United States are not found in other societies.
    (c)   Thinking globally is a good way to learn more about ourselves.
    (d)   All of the above are identified as reasons why a global perspective is so important.

6. The term *sociology* was coined in 1838 by

    (a)   Auguste Comte.
    (b)   Karl Marx.
    (c)   Herbert Spencer.
    (d)   Emile Durkheim.

7. According to Auguste Comte, the key to understanding society was to look at it

    (a)   using common sense.
    (b)   using intuition.
    (c)   theologically.
    (d)   metaphysically.
    (e)   scientifically.

8. *Positivism* is the idea that _____, rather than any other type of human understanding, is the path to knowledge.

    (a)   common sense
    (b)   science
    (c)   faith
    (d)   optimism

9. A *basic image* of society that guides thinking and research is the definition for

    (a)   a theoretical approach.
    (b)   manifest functions.
    (c)   social marginality.
    (d)   positivism.

10. Any relatively stable pattern of social behavior refers to

    (a)   social functions.
    (b)   theories.
    (c)   social structure.
    (d)   positivism.

11. Consequences of social structure that are largely *unrecognized* and *unintended* are called

    (a)   approaches.
    (b)   latent functions.
    (c)   manifest functions.
    (d)   social integration.

12.   *Structural-functionalism* has been criticized for

(a)   focusing too much attention on social conflict.
(b)   attending to questions concerning how life is experienced by individuals on a day-to-day basis, while ignoring larger social structures.
(c)   tending to ignore inequalities that can generate tension and conflict.
(d)   emphasizing the functional value of social change, while ignoring the integrative qualities of different social institutions.

13.   Which theoretical perspective is best suited for analysis using a *macro-level* orientation?

(a)   dramaturgical analysis
(b)   social exchange theory
(c)   symbolic-interactionist approach
(d)   ethnomethodology
(e)   social-conflict approach

14.   The questions "How is society experienced?" and, "How do individuals attempt to shape the reality perceived by others?" are most likely asked by a researcher following which theoretical approach?

(a)   structural-functional
(b)   symbolic-interaction
(c)   social Darwinism
(d)   social-conflict

15.   Sociology is not involved in *stereotyping* because

(a)   sociology makes generalizations about categories of people, not stereotypes.
(b)   sociologists base their generalizations on research.
(c)   sociologists strive to be fair-minded.
(d)   all of the above

Matching

1.   ____   The study of the larger world and our society's place in it.
2.   ____   A statement of how and why specific facts are related.
3.   ____   A framework for building theory based on the assumption that society is a complex system whose parts work together to promote solidarity and stability.
4.   ____   Relatively stable patterns of social behavior.
5.   ____   A framework for building theory that sees society as an arena of inequality that generates conflict and change.
6.   ____   A mental construct that represents an aspect of the world, inevitably in a somewhat simplified way.
7.   ____   An apparent, although false, relationship between two (or more) variables caused by some other variable.
8.   ____   A state of personal neutrality in conducting research.

a.	concept	e.	structural-functional approach
b.	theory	f.	spurious correlation
c.	social-conflict approach	g.	objectivity
d.	social structure	h.	global perspective

Fill-In

1. The systematic study of human society is the general definition for _____.
2. Emile Durkheim reasoned that the variation in *suicide rates* between different categories of people had to do with *social* _____.
3. The United States, Canada, and most of the nations of Western Europe are classified in terms of economic development as being the _____-*income countries.*
4. Important reasons for taking a *global perspective* include: where we live makes a great difference in _____ our lives, societies around the world are increasingly _____, many human problems that we face in the United States are far more _____ elsewhere, and it is a good way to learn more about _____.
5. Three changes are especially important to the development of sociology in Europe during the nineteenth century, including: a new _____ *economy*, a growth of _____, and _____ change.
6. A _____ is a statement of how and why specific facts are related.
7. _____ refers to two variables that *vary together*, such as the extent of crowding and juvenile delinquency.
8. The term _____ refers to a procedure for determining the value of a variable in a specific case.

Discussion

1. Differentiate between the concepts *manifest* and *latent functions* and provide an illustration for each.
2. Discuss Emile Durkheim's explanation of how *suicide rates* vary between different categories of people. Explain how this research demonstrates the application of the *sociological perspective.*
3. What are the three types of countries identified in the text as measured by their level of *economic development*? What are the characteristics of the countries that represent each of the three types?
4. What are the three major reasons why a *global perspective* is so important today?
5. What are the three major *theoretical approaches* used by sociologists? Identify two key questions raised by each in the analysis of society. Identify one weakness for each of these approaches for understanding the nature of human social life.
6. What are the four *benefits* of using the sociological perspective? Provide an illustration for two of these.
7. Based on what you have read in the text so far, what is your interpretation of *sociology* as a discipline of study?
8. What are two reasons why sociology is not to be considered nothing more than stereotyping?

PART VI: ANSWERS TO STUDY QUESTIONS

Key Concepts

1.   Sociology (p. 2)
2.   global perspective (p. 6)
3.   High-income (p. 6)
4.   middle-income (p. 6)
5.   low-income (p. 8)
6.   positivism (p. 10)
7.   theory (p. 11)
8.   theoretical approach (p. 11)
9.   structural-functional (p. 11)
10.   social structure (p. 11)
11.   social functions (p. 12)
12.   Manifest functions (p. 12)
13.   Latent functions (p. 12)
14.   social dysfunctions (p. 12)
15.   social-conflict (p. 12)
16.   macro-level (p. 13)
17.   micro-level (p. 13)
18.   symbolic-interaction (p. 14)
19.   Science (p. 15)
20.   concept (p. 15)
21.   Variables (p. 15)
22.   measurement (p. 15)
23.   Reliability (p. 15)
24.   Validity (p. 15)
25.   correlation (p. 15)
26.   cause and effect (p. 16)
27.   Interpretive sociology (p. 18)
28.   Critical sociology (p. 19)
29.   gender (p. 20)
30.   research method (p. 20)
31.   experiment (p. 20)
32.   survey (p. 22)
33.   Participant observation (p. 25)
34.   Stereotype (p. 29)

True-False

1.	F	(p. 2)	5.	F	(p. 12)
2.	T	(p. 6)	6.	T	(pp. 13-14)
3.	T	(pp. 8-9)	7.	T	(p. 19)
4.	T	(p. 11)	8.	T	(p. 20)

Multiple Choice

1.	c	(p. 2)	9.	a	(p. 11)
2.	d	(p. 3)	10.	c	(p. 11)
3.	a	(p. 4)	11.	b	(p. 12)
4.	a	(p. 8)	12.	d	(p. 12)
5.	b	(p. 8)	13.	e	(p. 13)
6.	a	(p. 10)	14.	b	(p. 14)
7.	e	(p. 10)	15.	d	(p. 29)
8.	b	(p. 10)			

Matching

1.	h	(p. 6)	5.	c	(p. 12)
2.	b	(p. 11)	6.	a	(p. 15)
3.	e	(p. 11)	7.	f	(p. 18)
4.	d	(p. 11)	8.	g	(p. 18)

Fill-In

1. sociology (p. 2)
2. integration (p. 4)
3. high (p. 6)
4. shaping, interconnected, serious, ourselves (p. 8)
5. industrial, cities, political (pp. 8-9)
6. theory (p. 11)
7. Correlation (pp. 15-16)
8. measurement (p. 15)

PART VII: IN FOCUS--IMPORTANT ISSUES

- The Sociological Perspective

  Define and illustrate each of the three *components of the sociological perspective.*

- The Importance of Global Perspective

  What are the four reasons why a *global perspective* is so important?

- The Origins of Sociology

  Auguste Comte saw sociology as the product of a three-stage historical development. **Define each of them.**

  > theological stage
  >
  > metaphysical stage
  >
  > scientific stage

- Sociological Theory

  Define each of the following *theoretical approaches*.

  > structural-functional
  >
  > social-conflict
  >
  > symbolic-interaction

- Scientific Sociology

  Define and illustrate each of the following *elements of science*.

  > concept
  >
  > variable
  >
  > measurement
  >
  > reliability
  >
  > validity
  >
  > correlation
  >
  > cause and effect
  >
  > objectivity

- Research Methods

  Describe each of the following research methods.

  experiment

  survey

  participant observation

Chapter 2   Culture

PART I: CHAPTER OUTLINE

PART II: LEARNING OBJECTIVES

- To begin to understand the sociological meaning of the concept of culture.
- To consider the relationship between human intelligence and culture.
- To know the components of culture and to provide examples of each.
- To identify the dominant values in our society and to recognize their interrelationships with one another and with other aspects of our culture.
- To explain how subcultures and countercultures contribute to cultural diversity.
- To begin to develop your understanding of multiculturalism.
- To differentiate between ethnocentrism and cultural relativism.
- To compare and contrast analyses of culture using structural-functional, social-conflict, and sociobiological approaches.
- To identify the consequences of culture for human freedom and constraint.

PART III: KEY CONCEPTS

1. The term _____ refers to the values, beliefs, behavior, and material objects that, together, form a people's way of life.
2. People who interact in a defined territory and share culture are known as a _____.
3. Going to another culture can cause _____ _____, or personal disorientation when experiencing another way of life.
4. A_____ is anything that carries a particular meaning recognized by people who share a culture.
5. A system of symbols that allows people to communicate with one another is known as a _____.
6. _____ _____ refers to the process by which one generation passes culture to the next.
7. The _____ _____ states that people perceive the world through the cultural lens of language.
8. _____ are culturally defined standards by which people assess desirability, goodness, and beauty and that serve as broad guidelines for social living.
9. _____ are specific statements that people hold to be true.
10. _____ refer to rules and expectations by which a society guides the behavior of its members.
11. Norms that are widely observed and have great moral significance are called _____.
12. _____ are norms for routine, casual interaction.
13. _____ refers to knowledge that people use to make a way of life in their surroundings.
14. The use of simple tools to hunt animals and gather vegetation is called _____ ____ _____.
15. _____ is the use of hand tools to raise crops.
16. The domestication of animals is known as _____.
17. Large-scale cultivation using plows harnessed to animals or more powerful energy sources is called _____.
18. _____ is defined as the production of goods using advanced sources of energy to drive large machinery.
19. Cultural patterns that distinguish a culture's elite are known as _____ _____.

14

20. _____ _____ refers to cultural patterns that are widespread among a society's population.

21. The term _____ refers to cultural patterns that set apart some segment of a society's population.

22. _____ is an educational program recognizing the cultural diversity of the United States and promoting the equality of all cultural traditions.

23. _____ refers to the dominance of European (especially English) cultural patterns.

24. _____ refers to the dominance of African cultural patterns.

25. A _____ refers to cultural patterns that strongly oppose those widely accepted within a society.

26. _____ _____ refers to the close relationships among various elements of a cultural system.

27. The fact that some cultural elements change more quickly than others, which may disrupt a cultural system, is known as _____ _____.

28. The practice of judging another culture by the standards of one's own culture is known as _____.

29. _____ _____ refers to the practice of evaluating a culture by its own standards.

30. Traits that are part of every known culture are referred to as _____ _____.

31. _____ is a theoretical approach that explores ways in which human biology affects how we create culture.

PART IV: IMPORTANT RESEARCHERS

In the space provided below each of the following researchers, write two or three sentences to help you remember his or her respective contributions to sociology.

Napoleon Chagnon

Edward Sapir and Benjamin Whorf

Charles Darwin

George Peter Murdock

Marvin Harris

Robin Williams

15

PART V: STUDY QUESTIONS

True-False

1. T   F   *Nonmaterial culture* refers to the intangible world of ideas created by members of a society.
2. T   F   The term *society* refers to a shared way of life.
3. T   F   *Values* are defined as rules and expectations by which society guides the behavior of its members.
4. T   F   *Mores* are norms that have little moral significance within a culture.
5. T   F   *Technology* is defined as the knowledge that people apply to the task of living in their surroundings.
6. T   F   We all participate in numerous subcultures without becoming very committed to them.
7. T   F   The practice of judging any culture by its own standards is referred to as *ethnocentrism*.
8. T   F   *Structural-functionalists* argue that there are no *cultural universals*.

Multiple Choice

1.   *Culture* is

   (a)   the process by which members of a culture encourage conformity to social norms.
   (b)   the beliefs, values, behavior, and material objects that constitute a people's way of life.
   (c)   the practice of judging another society's norms.
   (d)   a group of people who engage in interaction with one another on a continuous basis.

2.   The personal disorientation that accompanies exposure to an unfamiliar way of life is termed

   (a)   anomie.
   (b)   alienation.
   (c)   cultural relativism.
   (d)   culture shock.
   (e)   cultural transmission.

3.   The *Yanomamo* are

   (a)   a small tribal group of herders living in Eastern Africa.
   (b)   a technologically primitive horticultural society living in South America.
   (c)   a nomadic culture living above the Arctic circle as hunters.
   (d)   a small, dying society living as farmers in a mountainous region of western Africa.
   (e)   a people who until very recently were living in complete isolation from the rest of the world in a tropical rain forest in Malaysia.

4. Studying *fossil records*, scientists have concluded that the first creatures with clearly human characteristics, setting the human line apart from that of the great apes, existed about ___ years ago.

   (a)   2 million
   (b)   12 thousand
   (c)   40 million
   (d)   60 thousand
   (e)   12 million

5. *Homo sapiens* is a Latin term that means

   (a)   thinking person.
   (b)   to walk upright.
   (c)   evolving life form.
   (d)   dependent person.

6. The organized interaction of people in a nation or within some other boundary is the definition for

   (a)   culture.
   (b)   social structure.
   (c)   enculturation.
   (d)   socialization.
   (e)   society.

7. Which of the following identifies two of the *components of culture*?

   (a)   values and norms
   (b)   social change and social statics
   (c)   social structure and social function
   (d)   people and the natural environment

8. A system of *symbols* that allows members of a society to communicate with one another is the definition of

   (a)   language.
   (b)   cultural relativity.
   (c)   cultural transmission.
   (d)   values.

9. The *Sapir-Whorf thesis* relates to

   (a)   human evolution.
   (b)   language and cultural relativity.
   (c)   social sanctions.
   (d)   victimization patterns.

10. Culturally defined *standards* of desirability, goodness, and beauty, which serve as broad guidelines for social living, is the definition for

    (a)   norms.
    (b)   mores.
    (c)   beliefs.
    (d)   sanctions.
    (e)   values.

11. Progress and freedom are examples of U.S.

    (a)   norms.
    (b)   sanctions.
    (c)   values.
    (d)   beliefs.

12. Specific statements that people hold to be true refer to

    (a)   norms.
    (b)   values.
    (c)   sanctions.
    (d)   technology.
    (e)   beliefs.

13. Rules and expectations by which a society guides the behavior of is members refers to

    (a)   norms.
    (b)   values.
    (c)   sanctions.
    (d)   beliefs.

14. The old adage "Do as I say, not as I do" illustrates the distinction between

    (a)   ideal and real culture.
    (b)   the Sapir-Whorf hypothesis and "real" culture.
    (c)   cultural integration and cultural lag.
    (d)   folkways and mores.
    (e)   subcultures and countercultures.

15. Knowledge that people apply to the task of living in their surroundings refers to

    (a)   social control.
    (b)   technology.
    (c)   real culture.
    (d)   ideal culture.

Matching

1. ____ The intangible world of ideas created by members of society.
2. ____ Anything that carries a particular meaning recognized by people who share a culture.
3. ____ Rules and expectations by which a society guides the behavior of its members.
4. ____ Knowledge that people use to make a way of life in their surroundings.
5. ____ An educational program recognizing past and present diversity in U.S. society and promoting the equality of all cultural traditions.
6. ____ Cultural patterns that strongly oppose those widely accepted within a society.
7. ____ The fact that cultural elements change at different rates, which may disrupt a cultural system.
8. ____ The practice of judging another culture by the standards of one's own culture.

a. multiculturalism
b. counterculture
c. cultural lag
d. nonmaterial culture

e. technology
f. norms
g. symbol
h. ethnocentrism

Fill-In

1. _____ are the biological programming over which animals have no control.
2. While _____ are broad guidelines for social living, _____ are statements that people hold to be true.
3. Knowledge that people apply to the task of living in their surroundings refers to _____.
4. Sociologists use the term _____ *culture* to refer to cultural patterns that distinguish a society's elite; _____ *culture* designates cultural patterns that are widespread among a society's population.
5. _____ refers to an educational program recognizing the cultural diversity of the United States and promoting the equality of all cultural traditions.
6. Women's increased participation in the labor force parallels many changing family patterns, including first marriages at a later age and a rising divorce rate. Such patterns illustrate _____ _____, the close relationship among various elements of a cultural system.
7. The fact that some cultural elements change more quickly than others, which may disrupt a cultural system, is known as _____ _____.
8. Today, more than ever before, we can observe many of the same cultural practices the world over. This *global culture* is evidenced by the presence of a global _____, global _____, and global _____.

Discussion

1. What are the basic qualities of the *Yanomamo* culture? What factors do you think may explain why they are so aggressive? To what extent are you able to view these people from a *cultural relativistic* perspective?
2. What is the basic position being taken by *sociobiologists* concerning the nature of culture? What are three examples used by sociobiologists to argue that human culture is determined by biology? To what extent do you agree or disagree with their position? Explain.
3. What is the *Sapir-Whorf thesis*? What evidence supports it? What evidence is inconsistent with this hypothesis?

4. In what ways are we *globally connected?* Illustrate two of these.
5. Write a paragraph in which you express your opinions about the issue of multiculturalism in our society. Address the benefits of this perspective being suggested by proponents of multiculturalism, as well as the potential problems with this perspective suggested by its critics.
6. Provide two examples of how culture *constrains* us (limits our freedom).
7. What conclusions do you make about immigration concerning the data presented in *Figure 2-3?*
8. Review the list of *core values* of our culture in the United States. Rank order the ten identified in the text in terms of how important they are in our society from your point of view. What values, if any, do you believe should be included in the "top ten" list? Do you feel any of those listed should not be on the list?

PART VI: ANSWERS TO STUDY QUESTIONS

Key Concepts

1. culture (p.36)
2. society (p. 36)
3. culture shock (p.38)
4. symbol (p. 40)
5. language (p. 40)
6. Cultural transmission (p. 41)
7. Sapir-Whorf thesis (pp. 41-42)
8. Values (p. 43)
9. Beliefs (p. 43)
10. Norms (p. 44)
11. mores (p. 44)
12. Folkways (p. 44)
13. Technology (p. 44)
14. hunting and gathering (p. 45)
15. Horticulture (p. 45)
16. pastoralism (p. 45)
17. agriculture (p. 46)
18. Industry (p. 46)
19. high culture (p. 48)
20. Popular culture (p. 48)
21. subculture (p. 48)
22. Multiculturalism (p. 49)
23. Eurocentrism (p. 50)
24. Afrocentrism (p. 50)
25. counterculture (p. 51)
26. Cultural integration (p. 51)
27. cultural lag (p. 51)
28. ethnocentrism (p. 53)
29. Cultural relativism (p. 53)
30. cultural universals (p. 55)
31. Sociobiology (p. 56)

True-False

1.	T	(p. 36)	5.	T	(p. 44)
2.	F	(p. 36)	6.	T	(p. 48)
3.	F	(p. 43)	7.	F	(p. 53)
4.	F	(p. 44)	8.	F	(pp. 54-55)

Multiple Choice

1.	b	(p. 36)	9.	b	(pp. 41-42)
2.	d	(p. 38)	10.	e	(p. 43)
3.	b	(p. 39)	11.	c	(pp. 43-44)
4.	e	(p. 38)	12.	e	(p. 43)
5.	a	(p. 38)	13.	a	(p. 44)
6.	e	(p. 36)	14.	a	(p. 44)
7.	a	(pp. 39-44)	15.	b	(p. 44)
8.	a	(p. 40)			

Matching

1.	d	(p. 36)	5.	a	(p. 49)
2.	g	(p. 40)	6.	b	(p. 51)
3.	f	(p. 44)	7.	c	(p. 51)
4.	e	(p. 44)	8.	h	(p. 53)

Fill-In

1. Instincts (p. 38)
2. values, beliefs (p. 43)
3. technology (p. 44)
4. high, popular (p. 48)
5. Multiculturalism (p. 49)
6. cultural integration (p. 51)
7. cultural lag (p. 51)
8. economy, communication, migration (p. 54)

PART VII: IN FOCUS--IMPORTANT ISSUES

- What is Culture?

    Distinguish between material and nonmaterial culture.

- The Components of Culture

  Define and illustrate each of the following *components of culture.*

  - symbols

  - language

  - values

  - beliefs

  - norms

  - "ideal" and "real" cultures

- Technology and Culture

  Define and describe examples of each of the following levels of technology

  - hunting and gathering

  - horticulture and pastoralism

  - agriculture

  - industry

  - postindustrial information technology

- Cultural Diversity

  Identify and describe an example for each of the following terms.

  - counterculture

  - subculture

  - multiculturalism

  - cultural lag

  - ethnocentrism

  - cultural relativism

- Theoretical Analysis of Culture

  Briefly describe how each of the *theoretical approaches* helps us understand cultural uniformity diversity.

- Culture and Human Freedom

  In what ways does culture *constrain* us?

  In what ways does culture offer us *freedom*?

Chapter 3

Socialization: From Infancy to Old Age

PART II: LEARNING OBJECTIVES

- To become aware of the effects of social isolation on humans and other primates.
- To become aware of the key components of Sigmund Freud's model of personality.
- To identify and describe the four stages of Jean Piaget's cognitive development theory.
- To identify and describe the stages of moral development as identified by Lawrence Kohlberg.
- To analyze Carol Gilligan's critique of Kohlberg's moral development model.
- To identify and describe Erik H. Erikson's stages of personality development.
- To consider the contributions of George Herbert Mead to the understanding of personality development.
- To compare the spheres of socialization (family, school, etc.) in terms of their effects on an individual's socialization experiences.
- To begin to understand the cross-cultural and historical patterns of death and dying.

PART III: KEY CONCEPTS

1. _____ refers to the lifelong social experience by which people develop their human potential and learn culture.
2. A person's fairly consistent patterns of acting, thinking, and feeling refers to their _____.
3. According to Sigmund Freud, the _____ represents the human being's basic drives, which are unconscious and demand immediate satisfaction.
4. According to Sigmund Freud, the _____ is a person's conscious efforts to balance innate pleasure-seeking drives with the demands of society.
5. Freud's term for the cultural values and norms internalized by an individual is known as the _____.
6. The _____ stage refers to Piaget's term for the level of human development at which individuals experience the world only through their senses.
7. The _____ stage refers to Piaget's term for the level of human development at which individuals first use language and other symbols.
8. The _____ _____ stage refers to Piaget's term for the level of human development at which individuals first perceive causal connections in their surroundings.
9. The _____ _____ stage refers to Piaget's term for the level of human development at which individuals think abstractly and critically.
10. The _____ refers to George Herbert Mead's term for the part of an individual's personality composed of self-awareness and self-image.
11. The _____ _____ refers to Cooley's term for self-image based on how we think others see us.

12. _____ _____ are people – such as parents – who have special significance for socialization.

13. Mead used the term _____ _____ to refer to widespread cultural norms and values we use as a reference in evaluating ourselves.

14. A _____ _____ is a group whose members have interests, social position, and age in common.

15. _____ _____ refers to learning that helps a person achieve a desired position.

16. The _____ _____ refers to the impersonal communications aimed at a vast audience.

17. The study of aging and the elderly is called _____.

18. _____ is a form of social organization in which the elderly have the most wealth, power, and prestige.

19. Prejudice and discrimination against the elderly is called _____.

20. A _____ is a category of people with a common characteristic, usually their age.

21. A _____ _____ refers to a setting in which people are isolated from the rest of society and manipulated by an administrative staff.

22. _____ refers to radically changing an inmate's personality by carefully controlling the environment.

PART IV: IMPORTANT RESEARCHERS

In the space provided below each of the following researchers, write two or three sentences to help you remember his or her respective contributions to sociology.

Kingsley Davis

John Watson

Harry and Margaret Harlow

Sigmund Freud

Jean Piaget

Lawrence Kohlberg

Carol Gilligan

Erik H. Erikson

Charles Horton Cooley

George Herbert Mead

Elisabeth Kübler-Ross

PART V: STUDY QUESTIONS

True-False

1. T F John Watson was a nineteenth-century psychologist who argued that human behavior was largely determined by *heredity*.
2. T F The cases of *Anna* and *Genie* support the arguments made by naturalists that certain personality characteristics are determined by heredity.
3. T F Sigmund Freud envisioned *biological factors* as having little or no influence on personality development.
4. T F The *id* in Freud's psychoanalytic theory represents the human being's basic needs, which are unconscious and demand immediate satisfaction.
5. T F The first stage in Jean Piaget's *cognitive development* theory is referred to as the *preoperational stage*.
6. T F According to Carol Gilligan, taking a *rule-based* approach to moral reasoning is superior to taking a *person-based* approach.
7. T F George Herbert Mead refers to *taking the role of the other* as the interplay between the *I* and *me*.
8. T F According to Erik H. Erikson's theory of personality development, the first challenge faced in life is *intimacy* versus *isolation*.

Multiple Choice

1. _____ holds that behavior is not instinctual but learned.

   (a) The theory of natural selection
   (b) Behaviorism
   (c) Sociobiology
   (d) Evolutionary theory

2. The story of *Anna* illustrates the significance of _____ in personality development.

   (a) heredity
   (b) social interaction
   (c) physical conditions
   (d) ecology

3. What did the experiments on social isolation among rhesus monkeys show?

   (a) Artificial wire monkeys provided sufficient contact for young monkeys to develop normally.
   (b) The behavior of rhesus monkey infants is totally dissimilar to human infants.
   (c) Deprivation of social experience, rather than the absence of a specific parent, has devastating effects.
   (d) Genes found in rhesus monkeys cushion them from the negative effects of social isolation.

4. Which of the following is representative of *Sigmund Freud's* analysis of personality?

    (a)   Biological forces play only a small role in personality development.
    (b)   The term instinct is understood as very general human needs in the form of urges and drives.
    (c)   The most significant period for personality development is adolescence.
    (d)   Personality is best studied as a process of externalizing social forces.

5. Sigmund Freud theorized that humans have two basic needs: first, the need for bonding, which Freud called the life instinct, or *eros*; second, is an aggressive drive he called the *death instinct*, or

    (a)   storge.
    (b)   philos.
    (c)   agape.
    (d)   the superego.
    (e)   thanatos.

6. Culture existing within the individual was what *Sigmund Freud* called

    (a)   thanatos.
    (b)   eros.
    (c)   the ego.
    (d)   the id.
    (e)   the superego.

7. Jean Piaget's focus was on

    (a)   how children develop fine motor skills.
    (b)   how children are stimulated by their environment.
    (c)   cognition--how people think and understand.
    (d)   the role of heredity in determining human behavior.

8. According to *Jean Piaget*, which of the following best describes the *preoperational stage* of cognitive development?

    (a)   the level of human development in which the world is experienced only through sensory contact
    (b)   the level of human development characterized by the use of logic to understand objects and events
    (c)   the level of human development in which language and other symbols are first used
    (d)   the level of human development characterized by highly abstract thought

9. For a person operating at the *conventional stage* of Lawrence Kohberg's moral development theory,

   (a) "rightness" amounts to "what feels good to me."
   (b) an attempt is made to assess the intention in reaching moral judgments instead of simply observing what others do.
   (c) abstract ethical principles are applied, instead of using norms to make moral judgments.
   (d) moral decisions are based on avoidance of punishment.

10. According to research by Carol Gilligan, *males* use a _____ perspective concerning moral reasoning.

    (a) justice
    (b) independent
    (c) visual
    (d) mechanical

11 *George Herbert Mead's* perspective has often been described as

    (a) psychological pragmatism.
    (b) behaviorism.
    (c) social behaviorism.
    (d) psychoanalysis.
    (e) naturalism.

12 The concept of the *looking-glass self* refers to

    (a) Freud's argument that through psychoanalysis a person can uncover the unconscious.
    (b) Piaget's view that through biological maturation and social experience individuals become able to logically hypothesize about thoughts without relying on concrete reality.
    (c) Watson's behaviorist notion that one can see through to a person's mind only by observing the person's behavior.
    (d) Cooley's idea that the self-image we have is based on how we suppose others perceive us.

13. According to Erik H. Erikson, what is the challenge of *middle adulthood*?

    (a) integration versus despair
    (b) initiative versus guilt
    (c) industry versus inferiority
    (d) making a difference versus self-absorption

14. The process of social learning directed toward assuming a desired status and role in the future is called

    (a) resocialization.
    (b) socialization.
    (c) looking-glass self.
    (d) anticipatory socialization.

15.   Which of the following is *not* one of the three distinctive characteristics of a *total institution*?

    (a)   Staff members supervise all spheres of daily life.
    (b)   Staff members encourage the maintenance of individuality, and encourage creativity.
    (c)   Food, sleeping quarters, and activities are standardized.
    (d)   Formal rules dictate how virtually every moment is spent.

Matching

1. ____ A person's fairly consistent patterns of acting, thinking, and feeling.
2. ____ A theory developed by John Watson that holds that behavior patterns are not instinctive but learned.
3. ____ According to Sigmund Freud, the presence of culture within the individual.
4. ____ In Piaget's theory, the level of development at which individuals perceive causal connections in their surroundings.
5. ____ According to George Herbert Mead, the subjective side of the self.
6. ____ A group whose members have interests, social position, and age in common.
7. ____ Impersonal communications directed to a vast audience.
8. ____ A category of people with a common characteristic, usually their age.

    a.   behaviorism   e.   peer group
    b.   mass media   f.   personality
    c.   concrete operational stage   g.   superego
    d.   cohort   h.   I

Fill-In

1. The approach called _____ developed by *John Watson* in the early twentieth century provided a perspective that stressed learning rather than instincts as the key to personality development.
2. *Sigmund Freud* termed society's controlling influence on the drives of each individual as _____, whereas he called the process of transforming fundamentally selfish drives into more socially acceptable objectives _____.
3. According to Jean Piaget's theory of *cognitive development*, the level of human development at which individuals think abstractly and critically is known as the _____ _____ *stage*.
4. *Lawrence Kohlberg* identifies three stages in moral development. These include the _____, the _____, and the _____.
5. Carol Gilligan suggests that boys tend to use a *justice perspective* in moral reasoning, relying on formal rules in reaching a judgment about right and wrong. On the other hand, says Gilligan, girls tend to use a _____ and _____ *perspective* in moral reasoning, which leads them to judge a situation with an eye toward personal relationships.
6. *George Herbert Mead* explained that infants with limited social experience respond to others only in terms of _____.
7. According to Erik H. Erikson's developmental theory, the *challenge of adolescence* involves gaining _____ versus _____.
8. The process of social learning directed toward gaining a desired position is called _____ *socialization*.

<u>Discussion</u>

1. Review the research by *Harry* and *Margaret Harlow* on social isolation. What were the important discoveries they made?

2. Discuss the cases of *childhood isolation* presented in the text. What are the important conclusions being drawn from these cases?

3. What are the four stages of cognitive development according to *Jean Piaget*? Briefly describe the qualities of each stage. What is one major criticism of his theory?

4. What are the stages of personality development according to Erik H. Erikson? In what two important ways does his theory differ from Sigmund Freud's?

5. Define the concept *looking-glass self*. Provide an illustration from your own personal experience.

6. Define and differentiate between the terms *generalized other* and *significant other*. What are the four important *agents of socialization*? Provide an illustration of how each is involved in the socialization process.

7. What are the stages of *adulthood* and the qualities of each?

8. What is a *total institution*? What are the typical experiences of a person who is living within a total institution? How do these experiences affect personality development?

PART VI: ANSWERS TO STUDY QUESTIONS

<u>Key Concepts</u>

1. Socialization (p.64)
2. personality (p. 64)
3. id (p. 66)
4. ego (p. 66)
5. superego (p. 66)
6. sensorimotor (p. 67)
7. preoperational (p. 67)
8. concrete operations (p. 67)
9. formal operations (p. 67)
10. self (p. 68)
11. looking-glass self (p. 69)
12. Significant others (p. 69)
13. generalized other (p. 69)
14. peer group (p. 72)
15. Anticipatory socialization (p. 72)
16. mass media (p. 73)
17. gerontology (p. 77)
18. Gerontocracy (p. 78)
19. ageism (p. 78)
20. cohort (p. 80)
21. total institution (p. 81)
22. Resocialization (p. 80)

True-False

1.	F	(p. 65)	5.	F	(p. 67)
2.	F	(p. 66)	6.	F	(p. 68)
3.	F	(p. 66)	7.	T	(p. 69)
4.	T	(p. 66)	8.	F	(p. 70)

Multiple Choice

1.	b	(p. 65)	9.	b	(p. 68)
2.	b	(p. 66)	10.	a	(p. 68)
3.	c	(pp. 65-66)	11.	c	(p. 68)
4.	b	(p. 66)	12.	d	(p. 69)
5.	e	(p. 66	13.	d	(p. 70)
6.	e	(p. 66	14.	d	(p. 72)
7.	c	(p. 67	15.	b	(p. 81)
8.	c	(p. 67			

Matching

1.	f	(p. 64)	5.	h	(p. 69)
2.	a	(p. 65)	6.	e	(p. 72)
3.	g	(p. 66)	7.	b	(p. 73)
4.	c	(p. 67)	8.	d	(pp. 80-81)

Fill-In

1. behaviorism (p. 65)
2. repression, sublimation (pp. 66-67)
3. formal (p. 67)
4. preconventional, conventional, postconventional (p. 68)
5. care, responsibility (p. 68)
6. imitation (p. 69)
7. identity, confusion (p.70)
8. anticipatory (p.72)

PART VII: IN FOCUS—IMPORTANT ISSUES

• Social Experience: The Key to Our Humanity

According to Charles Darwin, what role does *nature* play in human personality development?

Review the conclusions being made by social scientists concerning the role of *nurture* in human personality development.

- Understanding Socialization

    Briefly review the major points being made by the following theorists concerning personality development. Identify and describe/define the stages of development for each theory discussed.

    Sigmund Freud

    Jean Piaget

    Lawrence Kohlberg

    Carol Gilligan

    George Herbert Mead

    Erik H. Erikson

- Agents of Socialization

    Briefly describe the significance for each of the following major agents of socialization on personality development.

    the family

    the school

    peer groups

    the mass media

- Socialization and the Life Course

    Identify two major points being made in the text concerning each of the following stages of the human life course.

    childhood

    adolescence

    adulthood

    old age

    dying

33

- Resocialization: Total Institutions

  What are the three major qualities of a *total institution*?

Chapter 4

Social Interaction in Everyday Life

PART I: CHAPTER OUTLINE

I. Social Structure: A Guide to Everyday Living
II. Status
    A. Ascribed Status and Achieved Status
    B. Master Status
III. Role
    A. Role Conflict and Role Strain
    B. Role Exit
IV. The Social Construction of Reality
    A. "Street Smarts"
    B. The Thomas Theorem
    C. Ethnomethodology
    D. Reality Building: Class and Culture
V. Dramaturgical Analysis: "The Presentation of Self"
    A. Performances
        1. An Application: The Doctor's Office
    B. Nonverbal Communication
        1. Body Language and Deception
    C. Gender and Performances
        1. Demeanor
        2. Use of Space
        3. Staring, Smiling, and Touching
    D. Idealization
    E. Embarrassment and Tact
VI. Interaction in Everyday Life: Three Applications
    A. Emotions: The Social Construction of Feeling
        1. The Biological Side of Emotions
        2. The Cultural Side of Emotions
        3. Emotions on the Job
    B. Language: The Social Construction of Gender
        1. Language and Power
        2. Language and Value
    C. Play: The Social Construction of Humor
        1. The Foundation of Humor
        2. The Dynamics of Humor: "Getting It"
        3. The Topics of Humor
        4. The Functions of Humor
        5. Humor and Conflict

PART II: LEARNING OBJECTIVES

- To identify the characteristics of social structure.
- To discuss the relationship between social structure and individuality.
- To distinguish among the different types of statuses and roles.
- To describe and illustrate the social construction of reality.
- To see the importance of performance, nonverbal communication, idealization, and embarrassment to the "presentation of the self."
- To describe and illustrate dramaturgical analysis.
- To understand the relationship between language and gender.
- To use gender and humor to illustrate how people construct meaning in everyday life.

PART III: KEY CONCEPTS

1. _____ _____ refers to the process by which people act and react in relation to others.

2. A _____ is a social position that a person occupies.

3. A _____ _____ refers to all the statuses a person holds at a given time.

4. An _____ _____ is a social position a person receives at birth or assumes involuntarily later in life.

5. An _____ _____ is a social position a person assumes voluntarily that reflects personal ability and effort.

6. A _____ _____ is a status that has special importance for social identity, often shaping a person's entire life.

7. A _____ refers to behavior expected of someone who holds a particular status.

8. A _____ _____ is a number of roles attached to a single status.

9. _____ _____ refers to conflict among roles corresponding to two or more statuses.

10. _____ _____ refers to conflict among roles connected to a single status.

11. The _____ _____ ____ _____ refers to the process by which people creatively shape reality through social interaction.

12. The _____ _____ refers to W.I. Thomas's assertion that situations that are defined as to be real are real in their consequences.

13. _____ is Harold Garfinkel's term for the study of the way people make sense of their everyday surroundings.

14. _____ _____ is Goffman's term for the study of social interaction in terms of theatrical performance.

15. The _____ ____ _____ refers to Goffman's term for an individual's efforts to create specific impressions in the minds of others.

36

16. _____ _____ refers to communication using body movements, gestures, and facial expressions rather than speech.

17. _____ _____ refers to the surrounding area over which a person makes some claim to privacy.

PART IV: IMPORTANT RESEARCHERS

In the space provided below each of the following researchers, write two or three sentences to help you remember his or her respective contributions to sociology.

Robert Merton   Harold Garfinkel

Erving Goffman   Paul Ekman

PART V: STUDY QUESTIONS

True-False

1.	T	F	A *status* refers to a pattern of expected behavior for individual members of society.
2	T	F	Both *statuses* and *roles* vary by culture.
3	T	F	Being an honors student, being a spouse, and being a computer programmer are examples of *ascribed statuses*.
4	T	F	*Role strain* refers to the incompatibility among roles corresponding to a single status.
5	T	F	The phrase *the social construction of reality* relates to the sociologist's view that statuses and roles structure our lives along narrowly delineated paths.
6.	T	F	According to Erving Goffman, *performances* are very rigidly scripted, leaving virtually no room for individual adaptation.
7.	T	F	According to research on gender and personal performances, men use significantly more space than women.
8.	T	F	Erving Goffman's research suggests that *tact* is relatively uncommon in our society.

Multiple Choice

1.   What is the term for a recognized social position that an individual occupies?

    (a)   prestige
    (b)   status
    (c)   social power
    (d)   role
    (e)   dramaturgy

2. What is the term for a status that has exceptional importance for social identity, often shaping a person's entire life?

   (a)   role
   (b)   ascribed status
   (c)   achieved status
   (d)   master status
   (e)   role set

3. What is the term for patterns of expected behavior attached to a particular status?

   (a)   role
   (b)   master status
   (c)   achieved status
   (d)   ascribed status
   (e)   performance

4. A number of roles attached to a single status refers to

   (a)   a role set.
   (b)   a status set.
   (c)   a master status.
   (d)   role conflict.
   (e)   role platform.

5. The incompatibility among the roles corresponding to two or more statuses refers to

   (a)   role conflict.
   (b)   role strain.
   (c)   status overload.
   (d)   status inconsistency.
   (e)   role set.

6. The *Thomas theorem* states that

   (a)   roles are only as important as the statuses to which they are attached.
   (b)   statuses are only as important as the roles on which they are dependent.
   (c)   the basis of humanity is built on the dual existence of creativity and conformity.
   (d)   common sense is only as good as the social structure within which it is embedded.
   (e)   situations defined as real become real in their consequences.

7. What is the term for the study of the way people make sense of their everyday lives?

   (a)   naturalism
   (b)   phenomenology
   (c)   ethnomethodology
   (d)   social psychology

8. The approach used by *ethnomethodologists* to study everyday interaction involves

   (a) conducting surveys.
   (b) unobtrusive observation.
   (c) secondary analysis.
   (d) breaking rules.
   (e) laboratory experiment.

9. The investigation of social interaction in terms of *theatrical performance* is referred to as

   (a) ethnomethodology.
   (b) dramaturgical analysis.
   (c) theatrical analysis.
   (d) phenomenology.

10. The process of the *presentation of the self* is also known as

    (a) ethnomethodology.
    (b) achieved status.
    (c) status consistency.
    (d) ascribed status.
    (e) impression management.

11. *Mr. Preedy*, the fictional character introduced in the text, provides an example of

    (a) role conflict.
    (b) role strain.
    (c) nonverbal communication.
    (d) status inconsistency.

12. According Paul Ekman, there are several *universal emotions*. Which of the following is *not* one he has identified?

    (a) hope
    (b) fear
    (c) sadness
    (d) happiness

13. Trying to convince others (and perhaps ourselves) that what we do reflects ideal cultural standards rather than selfish motives refers to

    (a) backstaging.
    (b) idealization.
    (c) ethnomethodology.
    (d) tact.

14.   Helping a person to "save face," or avoid embarrassment, is called

   (a)   diplomacy.
   (b)   generosity.
   (c)   altruism.
   (d)   tact.

15.   Which of the following is *not* a *function of humor*?

   (a)   Humor can be used to ease tension in uncomfortable situations.
   (b)   Humor limits racism and sexism.
   (c)   Humor can be a safety valve.
   (d)   Humor can be used to express feelings without being serious.

Matching

1.   ___   The process by which people act and react in relation to others.
2.   ___   A recognized social position that an individual occupies.
3.   ___   A social position a person receives at birth or assumes involuntarily later in life.
4.   ___   Expected behavior of someone who holds a particular status.
5.   ___   Incompatibility among roles corresponding to a single status.
6.   ___   Incompatibility among roles corresponding to two or more statuses.
7.   ___   Situations defined as real become real in their consequences.
8.   ___   The study of the way people make sense of their everyday lives.

   a.   ascribed status   e.   social interaction
   b.   ethnomethodology   f.   role
   c.   Thomas theorem   g.   status
   d.   role strain   h.   role conflict

Fill-In

1.   _____ _____ refers to the process by which people act and react in relation to others.

2.   _____ refers to a recognized social position that an individual occupies in society, while _____ refers to patterns of expected behaviors attached to a particular status.

3.   _____ refers to the incompatibility among the roles corresponding to two or more statuses.

4.   The _____ _____ suggests that situations that are defined as real are real in their consequences.

5.   The study of everyday, common-sense understandings that people within a culture have of the world around them is known as _____.

6.   Props in a doctor's office, like books and framed diplomas, are examples of the _____ *region* of the setting.

7. When people try to convince others that what they are doing reflects ideal cultural standards rather than less virtuous motives, Erving Goffman said they are involved in _____.

8. Language defines men and women differently in at least three ways--in terms of _____, _____, and _____.

Discussion

1. Review the story of the physician's office and *performances* in the text. Using this account as an example, select a social situation you have been involved in and do a dramaturgical analysis to describe its context.

2. Identify the types of information provided by a *performer* through nonverbal communication that can be used to determine whether or not a person is telling the truth. Provide illustrations.

3. What are three ways in which language functions to define the sexes differently? Provide an illustration for each of these.

4. What is *ethnomethodology*? Provide an illustration using your own example.

5. Define the concept *idealization*. Provide an illustration using the doctor's office account as a model.

6. Provide an example of the *Thomas theorem* using your own experiences either at home or in school.

7. What are the basic characteristics of *humor*? Write out a joke and analyze how it manifests the characteristics discussed in the text.

8. Create a two-person dialogue between a woman and a man that illustrates Deborah Tannen's points concerning the different languages of males and females.

PART VI: ANSWERS TO STUDY QUESTIONS

Key Concepts

1. Social interaction (p. 88)
2. status (p. 89)
3. status set (p. 89)
4. ascribed status (p. 89)
5. achieved status (p. 89)
6. master status (p. 89)
7. role (p. 90)
8. role set (p. 90)
9. Role conflict (p. 90)
10. Role strain (p. 90)
11. social construction of reality (p. 92)
12. Thomas theorem (p. 93)
13. Ethnomethodology (p. 93)
14. Dramaturgical analysis (p. 95)
15. presentation of self (p. 95)
16. Nonverbal communication (p. 96)
17. Personal space (p. 98)

True-False

1.	F	(p. 89)	5.	F	(p. 92)
2.	T	(p. 90)	6.	F	(p. 95)
3.	F	(p. 89)	7.	T	(p. 98)
4.	T	(p. 90)	8.	F	(pp. 98-99)

Multiple Choice

1.	b	(p. 89)	9.	b	(p. 95)
2.	d	(p. 89)	10.	e	(p. 95)
3.	a	(p. 90)	11.	c	(p. 96)
4.	a	(p. 90)	12.	a	(p. 99)
5.	a	(p. 90)	13.	b	(p. 98)
6.	e	(p. 93)	14.	d	(p. 99)
7.	c	(p. 93)	15.	b	(p. 103)
8.	d	(p. 94)			

Matching

1.	e	(p. 88)	5.	d	(p. 90)
2.	g	(p. 89)	6.	h	(p. 90)
3.	a	(p. 89)	7.	c	(p. 93)
4.	f	(p. 90)	8.	b	(p. 93)

Fill-In

1. Social interaction (p. 88)
2. Status, role (pp. 89-90)
3. Role conflict (p. 90)
4. Thomas theorem (p. 93)
5. ethnomethodology (p. 93)
6. back (p. 95)
7. idealization (p. 98)
8. power, value, attention (pp. 101-102)

PART VII: IN FOCUS—IMPORTANT ISSUES

- Social Structure: A Guide to Everyday Living

    Provide an illustration to support the point being made by the author that members of every society rely on social structure to make sense out of everyday situations.

- Status

    Outline your current *status set.*

- Role

    Provide an example for each of the following from your own life.

        role strain

        role conflict

        role exit

- The Social Construction of Reality

    Provide an illustration (from your own experience) of the *Thomas theorem.*

- Dramaturgical Analysis: "The Presentation of Self"

    Define and illustrate each of the following.

        performance

        nonverbal communication

        gender and performances (demeanor, use of space, staring, smiling, and touching)

        idealization

        embarrassment and tact

- Interaction in Everyday Life: Two Applications

  Language defines men and women differently. Illustrate how for each of the following ways this is true.

    power

    value

  Identify and illustrate three major *functions of humor*.

  What is the relationship between *humor and conflict*? Provide two illustrations.

Chapter

5

Groups and Organizations

PART I: CHAPTER OUTLINE

I.   Social Groups
    A.   Primary and Secondary Groups
    B.   Group Leadership
        1.   Instrumental and Expressive Leaders
        2.   Leadership Styles
    C.   Group Conformity
        1.   Asch's Research
        2.   Milgram's Research
        3.   Janis's Research
    D.   Reference Groups
        1.   Stouffer's Research
    E.   In-groups and Out-groups
    F.   Group Size
    G.   Social Diversity: Race, Class, and Gender
    H.   Networks

II.   Formal Organizations
    A.   Types of Formal Organizations
    B.   Origins of Bureaucracy
    C.   Characteristics of Bureaucracy
    D.   Organizational Environment
    E.   The Informal Side of Bureaucracy
    F.   Problems of Bureaucracy
        1.   Bureaucratic Alienation
        2.   Bureaucratic Inefficiency and Ritualism
        3.   Bureaucratic Inertia
        4.   Oligarchy

III.   The Evolution of Formal Organizations
    A.   Scientific Management
    B.   The First Challenge: Race and Gender
        1.   Patterns of Privilege and Exclusion
        2.   The "Female Advantage"
    C.   The Second Challenge: The Japanese Work Organization

PART II: LEARNING OBJECTIVES

- To identify the differences between primary groups and secondary groups.
- To identify the various types of leaders associated with social groups.
- To recognize the importance of reference groups to group dynamics.
- To distinguish between in-groups and out-groups.
- To understand the relevance of group size to the dynamics of social groups.
- To identify the types of formal organizations.
- To identify and describe the basic characteristics of bureaucracy.
- To become aware of both the limitations and informal side of bureaucracy.
- To identify and discuss three important challenges of the scientific management organizational model.
- To consider the issue of the "McDonaldization" of society.
- To analyze the two opposing trends concerning the future of organizations.

PART III: KEY CONCEPTS

1. A _____ _____ refers to two or more people who identify and interact with one another.
2. A small social group whose members share personal and enduring relationships is known as a _____ _____.
3. A large and impersonal group whose members pursue a specific goal or activity is known as a _____ _____.
4. _____ _____ refers to group leadership that emphasizes the completion of tasks.
5. _____ _____ refers to group leadership that focuses on collective well-being.
6. _____ refers to the tendency of group members to conform, resulting in a narrow view of some issue.
7. A _____ _____ is a social group that serves as a point of reference in making evaluations and decisions.
8. An _____ is a social group commanding a member's esteem and loyalty.
9. A social group toward which one feels competition or opposition is known as an _____.
10. A _____ is a social group with two members.
11. A _____ is a social group with three members.
12. A web of social ties is known as a _____.
13. A _____ _____ is a large secondary group organized to achieve its goals efficiently.

46

14. Sentiments and beliefs that are passed from generation to generation are called _____.
15. _____ refers to deliberate, matter-of-fact calculation of the most effective means to accomplish a particular task.
16. Max Weber used the term _____ _____ _____ to describe the historical change from tradition to rationality as the dominant mode of human thought.
17. A _____ is an organizational model rationally designed to perform tasks efficiently.
18. The _____ _____ refers to factors outside an organization that affects its operations.
19. _____ _____ refers to a preoccupation with rules and regulations to the point of thwarting an organization's goals.
20. _____ _____ refers to the tendency of bureaucratic organizations to perpetuate themselves.
21. An _____ refers to the rule of the many by the few.
22. _____ _____ refers to Frederick Taylor's term for the application of scientific principles to the operation of a business or other large organization.

PART IV: IMPORTANT RESEARCHERS

In the space provided below each of the following researchers, write two or three sentences to help you remember his or her respective contributions to sociology.

Max Weber   Georg Simmel

Charles Horton Cooley   Amitai Etzioni

Stanley Milgram   Solomon Asch

Irving Janis   Samuel Stouffer

Rosabeth Moss Kanter   Robert Michels

William Ouchi   Deborah Tannen

Sally Helgesen   Frederick Winslow Taylor

PART V: STUDY QUESTIONS

True-False

1.   T   F   Any collection of individuals can be called a *group*.
2.   T   F   *Expressive leadership* emphasizes the completion of tasks.
3.   T   F   *Networks* tend to be more enduring and provide a greater sense of identity than most other types of social groups.
4.   T   F   The *organizational environment* includes economic and political trends.
5.   T   F   *Bureaucratic inertia* refers to a preoccupation with rules and regulations to the point of thwarting an organization's goals
6.   T   F   According to research by Deborah Tannen, a "female advantage" for organizations is that women have a greater *information focus* than men.
7.   T   F   According to research by William Ouchi, formal organizations in Japan tend to be characterized by greater *holistic involvement* than those in the United States.
8.   T   F   A basic organizational principle involved in the *McDonaldization of society* is efficiency.

Multiple Choice

1. People who have some status in common, such as teachers, exemplify a

    (a)   social group.
    (b)   category.
    (c)   crowd.
    (d)   status set.

2. Which of the following is *not* true of *primary groups*?

    (a)   They provide security for their members.
    (b)   They are focused around specific activities.
    (c)   They are valued in and of themselves.
    (d)   They are viewed as ends in themselves.

3. Which of the following is *not* a characteristic of a *secondary group*?

    (a)   large size
    (b)   weak emotional ties
    (c)   personal orientation
    (d)   variable, often short duration

4.   What is the term for a *group leadership* that emphasizes the completion of tasks?

     (a)   task group leadership
     (b)   secondary group leadership
     (c)   expressive leadership
     (d)   instrumental leadership
     (e)   laissez-faire leadership

5.   Which of the following is *not* identified in the text as a *leadership style*?

     (a)   laissez-faire
     (b)   democratic
     (c)   authoritarian
     (d)   utilitarian

6.   Solomon Asch's classic investigation of group dynamics revealed the dramatic effects of

     (a)   leadership styles.
     (b)   leadership types.
     (c)   triads.
     (d)   group conformity.
     (e)   networking.

7.   Which researcher concluded that people are not likely to question authority figures even though common sense dictates that they should?

     (a)   Solomon Asch
     (b)   David Klein
     (c)   Stanley Milgram
     (d)   Charles Horton Cooley

8.   What is the sociological term for a limited understanding of some issue due to group conformity?

     (a)   conformist cognizance
     (b)   groupthink
     (c)   doublethink
     (d)   red tape

9.   A social group commanding a member's esteem and loyalty is a(n)

     (a)   ingroup.
     (b)   outgroup.
     (c)   reference group.
     (d)   subculture.
     (e)   residual group.

10. What types of *formal organizations* bestow material benefits on their members?

(a) normative organizations
(b) coercive organizations
(c) social organizations
(d) utilitarian organizations

11. What term refers to an *organizational model* rationally designed to perform complex tasks efficiently?

(a) bureaucracy
(b) complex organization
(c) humanized organization
(d) social organization

12. Which of the following is *not* part of the *organizational environment*?

(a) economic trends
(b) political trends
(c) population patterns
(d) other organizations
(e) company employees

13. *Bureaucratic ritualism* refers to

(a) the process of promoting people to their level of incompetence.
(b) the tendency of bureaucratic organizations to persist over time.
(c) the rule of the many by the few.
(d) a preoccupation with rules and regulations to the point of thwarting an organization's goals.
(e) the tendency for formal organizations to become more humanized as membership becomes more diversified.

14. Research by Deborah Tannen on gender and management styles has found that *men* tend to have a(n)

(a) image focus.
(b) information focus.
(c) flexibility focus.
(d) developmental focus.
(e) historical focus.

15. According to *William Ouchi* which of the following lists of qualities highlight the distinctions between formal organizations in Japan and the United States?

(a) hiring and advancement, lifetime security, holistic involvement, nonspecialized training, and collective decision making
(b) predictability, calculability, control through automation, and efficiency
(c) oligarchy, ritualism, privacy, and alienation
(d) competence, tasks, inertia, and networks
(e) productivity, developmental focus, physical plant characteristics

Matching

1. ___ Two or more people who identify and interact with one another.
2. ___ Large and impersonal groups based on a specific interest or activity.
3. ___ Group leaders who emphasize the completion of tasks.
4. ___ The tendency of group members to conform by adopting a narrow view of some issue.
5. ___ A social group that serves as a point of reference in making evaluations or decisions.
6. ___ A social group with two members.
7. ___ Large, secondary groups that are organized to achieve their goals efficiently.
8. ___ An organizational model rationally designed to perform complex tasks efficiently.

a. secondary group   e. social group
b. formal organization   f. reference group
c. groupthink   g. dyad
d. instrumental leaders   h. bureaucracy

Fill-In

1. A _____ _____ is defined as two or more people who identify and interact with one another.
2. While *primary* relationships have a _____ orientation, *secondary* relationships have a _____ orientation.
3. _____ *leadership* refers to group leadership that emphasizes the completion of tasks.
4. _____ *leaders* focus on instrumental concerns, make decisions on their own, and demand strict compliance from subordinates.
5. Amitai Etzioni has identified three *types of formal organizations*, distinguished by why people participate in them. Ones that pay their members are called _____ organizations. People become members of _____ organizations to pursue goals they consider morally worthwhile. Finally, _____ organizations are distinguished by involuntary membership.
6. *Deborah Tannen's* research on management styles suggests that women have a greater _____ *focus* and men have greater _____ *focus*.
7. Several ways in which today's *organizations* differ from those of a century ago are identified in the text, including: greater creative _____ for skilled workers, more use of _____ work teams, a _____ organizational structure, and greater _____ .

8. The four characteristics of the *McDonaldization of society* include _____, _____, _____ and _____, and _____ *through automation*.

Discussion

1. Differentiate between the qualities of *bureaucracies* and *small groups*. In what ways are they similar?
2. What are the three factors in decision-making processes in groups that lead to *groupthink*?
3. What are three major *limitations* of bureaucracy? Define and provide an illustration for each. What is meant by questioning "is rationality *irrational*"?
4. In what ways do bureaucratic organizations in *Japan* differ from those in the *U.S.*? What are the consequences of these differences? Relate this comparison to the issue of *humanizing* organizations.
5. Identify the basic *types of leadership* in groups and provide examples of the relative advantages and disadvantages for each type.
6. What are the general characteristics of the *McDonaldization* of society? Provide an illustration of this phenomenon in our society based on your own experience.
7. What are Peter Blau's major points concerning how the structure of social groups regulates intergroup association?
8. What are the three *types of organizations* identified by Amitai Etzioni? Describe and provide an illustration for each. From your own experience, illustrate two of the *characteristics of bureaucracy*— specifying which of Etzioni's type or types of organizations are being represented.

PART VI: ANSWERS TO STUDY QUESTIONS

Key Concepts

1. social group (p. 110)
2. primary group (p. 111)
3. secondary group (p. 111)
4. Instrumental leadership (p. 112)
5. Expressive leadership (p. 112)
6. Groupthink (p. 114)
7. reference group (p. 114)
8. in-group (p. 115)
9. out-group (p. 115)
10. dyad (p. 115)
11. triad (p. 116)
12. network (p. 116)
13. formal organization (p. 118)
14. tradition (p. 119)
15. Rationality (p. 119)
16. rationalization of society (p. 119)
17. bureaucracy (p. 120)
18. organizational environment (p. 121)
19. Bureaucratic ritualism (p. 122)
20. Bureaucratic inertia (p. 123)
21. oligarchy (p. 123)
22. Scientific management (p. 123)

True-False

1.	F	(p. 110)	5.	F	(pp. 122-123)
2.	F	(p. 112)	6.	T	(pp. 124-125)
3.	F	(pp. 116-117)	7.	T	(p. 125)
4.	T	(pp. 120-121)	8.	T	(p. 128)

Multiple Choice

1.	b	(p. 110)	9.	a	(p. 115)
2.	b	(pp. 111-112)	10.	d	(p. 119)
3.	c	(pp. 111-112)	11.	a	(p. 120)
4.	d	(p. 112)	12.	e	(pp. 120-121)
5.	d	(pp. 112-113)	13.	d	(p. 122)
6.	d	(p. 113)	14.	a	(pp. 124-125)
7.	c	(pp. 113-114)	15.	a	(p. 125)
8.	b	(p. 114)			

Matching

1.	e	(p. 110)	5.	f	(p. 114)
2.	a	(p. 111)	6.	g	(p. 115)
3.	d	(p. 112)	7.	b	(p. 118)
4.	c	(p. 114)	8.	h	(p. 120)

Fill-In

1. social group (p. 110)
2. personal, goal (p. 111)
3. Instrumental (p. 112)
4. Authoritarian (p. 112)
5. utilitarian, normative, coercive (p. 119)
6. information, image (p. 124)
7. autonomy, competitive, flatter, flexibility (p. 126)
8. efficiency, calculability, uniformity, predictability, control (pp. 128-129)

PART VII: IN FOCUS—IMPORTANT ISSUES

- Social Groups

  Define and illustrate each of the following.

    category

    crowd

primary group

secondary group

Define and provide an example for each of the following *types of leadership*.

instrumental leadership

expressive leadership

Describe each of the following *leadership styles*.

authoritarian leadership

democratic leadership

laissez-faire leadership

Describe the research procedures and findings/conclusions for each of the following researcher's work on *group conformity*.

Asch's research

Milgram's research

Janis's research

Identify and describe the three ways in which *social diversity* influences intergroup contact as outlined by Peter Blau.

What is a *network*? How do networks differ for men and women?

- Formal Organizations

    What is a *formal organization*?

    Define and illustrate the different *types* of formal organizations

    What is meant by the term *bureaucracy?*

    Max Weber identified six *key elements* of the ideal bureaucratic organization. Define and illustrate each of these elements.

    Identify two examples of the *informal side of bureaucracy.*

    Identify and describe three major *problems of bureaucracy.*

- The Evolution of Formal Organizations

    What are the three steps involved in *scientific management?*

    What are the major characteristics of the *"McDonaldization" of society?* Provide evidence for the existence of each in our society today.

- The Future of Organizations: Opposing Trends

    What are the two *opposing tendencies* identified by the author?

Chapter 6 — Sexuality and Society

PART I: CHAPTER OUTLINE

I. Understanding Sexuality
   A. Sex: A Biological Issue
   B. Sex and the Body
      1. Intersexual People
      2. Transsexuals
   C. Sex: A Cultural Issue
      1. Cultural Variation
   D. The Incest Taboo
II. Sexual Attitudes in the United States
   A. The Sexual Revolution
   B. The Sexual Counterrevolution
   C. Premarital Sex
   D. Sex between Adults
   E. Extramarital Sex
   F. Sexual Orientation
   G. What Gives Us A Sexual Orientation?
      1. Sexual Orientation: A Product of Society
      2. Sexual Orientation: A Product of Biology
   H. How Many Gay People Are There?
   I. The Gay Rights Movement
III. Sexual Controversies
   A. Teen Pregnancy
   B. Pornography
   C. Prostitution
      1. Types of Prostitution
      2. A Victimless Crime?
   D. Sexual Violence: Rape and Date Rape
      1. Rape
      2. Date Rape
IV. Theoretical Analysis of Sexuality
   A. Structural-Functional Analysis
      1. The Need to Regulate Sexuality
      2. Latent Functions: The Case of Prostitution
   B. Symbolic-Interaction Analysis
      1. The Social Construction of Sexuality
      2. Global Comparisons
   C. Social-Conflict Analysis
      1. Sexuality: Reflecting Social Inequality
      2. Sexuality: Creating Social Inequality
      3. Queer Theory

PART II: LEARNING OBJECTIVES

- To gain a sociological understanding of human sexuality focusing on both biological and cultural factors.
- To become more aware of the sexual attitudes found in the United States today.
- To describe both the sexual revolution and sexual counterrevolution that occurred during the last half century in the United States.
- To discuss issues relating to the biological and social causes of sexual orientation.
- To gain a sociological perspective on several sexual controversies, including teen pregnancy, pornography, prostitution, and sexual violence and abuse.
- To discuss issues relating to human sexuality from the viewpoints offered by structural-functional, symbolic-interactionist, and social-conflict analysis.

PART III: KEY CONCEPTS

Fill in the blank spaces below with the appropriate concepts.

1.   _____ refers to the biological distinction between females and males.
2.   The genitals—or organs used for reproduction—refer to _____ _____ _____.
3.   _____ _____ _____ refer to bodily differences, apart from the genitals, that distinguishes biologically mature females and males.
4.   _____ _____ are human beings whose bodies (including genitals) have both female and male characteristics.
5.   _____ are people who feel they are one sex even though biologically they are the other.
6.   An _____ _____ is a norm forbidding sexual relations or marriage between certain relatives.
7.   _____ _____ refers to a person's romantic and emotional attraction to another person.
8.   _____ is a sexual orientation in which a person is sexually attracted to someone of the other sex.
9.   _____ is a sexual orientation in which a person is sexually attracted to someone of the same sex.
10.   _____ is a sexual orientation in which a person is sexually attracted to people of both sexes.
11.   _____ is a sexual orientation in which a person is not sexually attracted to people of either sex.
12.   The dread of close personal interaction with people thought to be gay, lesbian, or bisexual refers to _____.
13.   _____ refers to sexually explicit material that causes sexual arousal.
14.   The selling of sexual services is known as _____.

15. _____ _____ is a growing body of research findings that challenges the heterosexual bias in U.S. society.

16. _____ refers to a view stigmatizing anyone who is not heterosexual as "queer."

17. _____ refers to the deliberate termination of a pregnancy.

PART IV: IMPORTANT RESEARCHERS

In the space provided below each of the following researchers, write two or three sentences to help you remember his or her respective contributions to the field of sociology.

Alfred Kinsey   Helen Colton

Simon LeVay   Kingsley Davis

PART V: STUDY QUESTIONS

True-False

1. T F In *fertilization*, the male contributes either an X or Y chromosome.
2. T F *Primary sex characteristics* are those that develop during puberty.
3. T F One cultural universal—an element found in every society the world over—is the *incest taboo*.
4. T F *Sexual orientation* refers to the biological distinction of being female or male.
5. T F Most research indicates that among *homosexuals*, lesbians outnumber gays by a ratio of about two-to-one.
6. T F *Pornography* refers to sexually explicit material that causes sexual arousal.
7. T F Among the types of *prostitutes*, call girls have the lowest status.
8. T F According to national survey research, over one-third of adults in the U.S. think that a woman should be able to obtain a legal *abortion* for any reason if she wants to.

Multiple Choice

1. _____ refers to the biological distinction between females and males.

   (a)   Gender
   (b)   Sex
   (c)   Sexual orientation
   (d)   Human sexuality

2. In reproduction, a female ovum and a male sperm, each containing_____ chromosomes, combine to form a fertilized embryo. One of these chromosome pairs determines the child's sex.

   (a)   12
   (b)   7
   (c)   23
   (d)   31

3. _____ are people who feel they are one sex even though biologically they are of the other sex.

    (a)   Intersexual people
    (b)   Transvestites
    (c)   Homophobics
    (d)   Transsexuals

4. If an Islamic woman is disturbed by another person while she is bathing, what body part is she most likely to cover?

    (a)   her feet
    (b)   her breasts
    (c)   her navel
    (d)   her genitals
    (e)   her face

5. According to the _____, society allows (and even encourages) men to be sexually active, while expecting women to remain chaste before marriage and faithful to their husbands afterwards.

    (a)   sexual counterrevolution
    (b)   sexual revolution
    (c)   double-standard
    (d)   permissiveness index

6. Approximately _____ *percent* of U.S. adults say that premarital sexual intercourse is "always wrong."

    (a)   20
    (b)   35
    (c)   15
    (d)   60
    (e)   8

7. _____ refers to a person's romantic and emotional attraction to another person.

    (a)   Sexual orientation
    (b)   Sex
    (c)   Gender
    (d)   Sexual response

8. According to the Laumann survey, approximately _____ percent of men and _____ percent of women in the U.S. define themselves as partly or entirely *homosexual*.

    (a)   10.4; 12.4
    (b)   12.1; 8.7
    (c)   6.5; 7.0
    (d)   11.3; 2.6
    (e)   2.8; 1.4

9. Which of the following are accurate concerning *teen pregnancy* in the United States?

   (a) Approximately one million teens become pregnant each year.
   (b) Most teens who get pregnant did not intend to.
   (c) Teens who become pregnant are at great risk of poverty.
   (d) The U.S. has a higher rate of teen pregnancy than that found in other industrial societies.
   (e) All of the above are accurate.

10. Which of the following statements reflects the current position of the Supreme Court of the United States regarding *pornography*?

   (a) The Court has never made a ruling concerning pornography.
   (b) The Court has established federal guidelines regarding what material is to be considered pornographic.
   (c) The Court's ruling has given local communities the power to decide for themselves what violates "community standards" of decency and lacks any redeeming social value.
   (d) The Court has ruled the First Amendment to the United States Constitution forbids any legal definitions for pornography.

11. Which of the following is *inaccurate* about *prostitution*?

   (a) Most prostitutes are women.
   (b) Most prostitutes offer heterosexual services.
   (c) Call girls are the lowest prestige type of prostitution.
   (d) Prostitution is greatest in poor countries where patriarchy is strong and traditional cultural norms limit women's ability to earn a living.

12. *Prostitution* is classified as being what type of crime?

   (a) property
   (b) victimless
   (c) white-collar
   (d) violent

13. Which of the following is *inaccurate* concerning the *structural-functional* approach to sexuality?

   (a) It helps us to appreciate how sexuality plays an important part in how society is organized.
   (b) It focuses attention on how societies, through the incest taboo and other cultural norms, have always paid attention to who has sex with whom, especially who reproduces with whom.
   (c) This approach pays considerable attention to the great diversity of sexual ideas and practices found around the world.
   (d) All of the above are accurate.

14. Which of the following is a criticism of the *symbolic-interactionist* approach to sexuality.

   (a) It fails to take into account how social patterns regarding sexuality are socially constructed.
   (b) It fails to help us appreciate the variety of sexual practices found over the course of history and around the world.
   (c) It fails to identify the broader social structures that establish certain patterns of sexual behaviors cross-culturally.
   (d) None of the above is a criticism of symbolic-interactionism.

15. *Queer theory* is most likely accepted by proponents of which of the following approaches?

   (a) structural-functionalists
   (b) symbolic-interactionsists
   (c) social-conflict theorists
   (d) none of the above

Matching

1. ___ The biological distinction between females and males.
2. ___ The genitals, organs used for reproduction.
3. ___ People who feel they are one sex even though biologically they are of the other.
4. ___ No sexual attraction to people of either sex.
5. ___ Sexual attraction to people of both sexes.
6. ___ The selling of sexual services.
7. ___ A view stigmatizing anyone who is not heterosexual as "queer."
8. ___ Refers to a growing body of knowledge that challenges heterosexism.

   a. transsexuals   e. heterosexism
   b. queer theory   f. prostitution
   c. asexuality   g. bisexuality
   d. primary sex characteristics h. sex

Fill-In

1. _____ *sex characteristics* refer to bodily differences, apart from the genitals, that distinguish biologically mature females and males.
2. Human beings with some combination of female and male characteristics (including genitals) are referred to as _____ _____.
3. One cultural universal--an element found in every society the world over--is the _____ _____, a norm forbidding sexual relations or marriage between certain relatives.
4. Given current scientific research evidence, the best guess at present is that *sexual orientation* is derived from both _____ and _____.
5. Recent research suggests that about _____ percent of U.S. *males* and _____ percent of U.S. *females* aged between eighteen and fifty-nine reported *homosexual activity* at some time in their lives.
6. _____ describes the dread of close personal interaction with people thought to be gay, lesbian, or bisexual.
7. Traditionally, people have criticized *pornography* on _____ grounds. Today, however, pornography is seen as a _____ issue because it depicts women as the sexual playthings of men.

61

8.   At the bottom of the *sex-worker hierarchy* are _____ _____.

Discussion

1.   What evidence was used by Alfred Kinsey to suggest considerable *cultural variation* exists in terms of sexual practices? What does Alfred Kinsey mean by the *sexual orientation continuum*? What are the data he uses to argue for its existence?
2.   What are the functions served by the *incest taboo* for both individuals and society as a whole?
3.   What does the author mean by saying that sexual attitudes in the United States are both *restrictive* and *permissive*? When was the *sexual revolution*? What social and cultural factors influenced this revolution? What was the *sexual counterrevolution*? What social and cultural factors helped bring it about? How would you summarize our society's attitudes concerning *premarital sex*?
4.   What is the evidence that sexual orientation is a *product of society*? What is the evidence that it is a *product of biology*?
5.   Why do you think *teen pregnancy* rates are higher in the United States than in other modern industrial societies? What are your opinions regarding *sex education* in the schools? What is the evidence for its effectiveness?
6.   To what extent would you agree that *pornography* today is less a moral issue than it is an issue concerning power? Why?
7.   Is *prostitution* really a victimless crime? Why? What are the *functions* of prostitution for society?
8.   What evidence do symbolic-interactionists use to suggest sexuality is *socially constructed*? Social-conflict theorists argue that sexuality is at the root of *inequality* between women and men. How is this so? Further, using each of these approaches, discuss the problem of *sexual violence* in our society. Why is sexual violence so prevalent in our society?

PART VI: ANSWERS TO STUDY QUESTIONS

Key Concepts

1.   Sex (p. 136)
2.   primary sex characteristics (p. 137)
3.   Secondary sex characteristics (p. 137)
4.   Intersexual people (p. 138)
5.   Transsexuals (p. 138)
6.   incest taboo (p. 139)
7.   Sexual orientation (p 143).
8.   Heterosexuality (p. 143)
9.   Homosexuality (pp. 143-144)
10.   Bisexuality (p. 144)
11.   Asexuality (p. 144)
12.   homophobia (p. 146)
13.   Pornography (p. 147)
14.   prostitution (p. 148)
15.   Queer theory (p. 155)
16.   Heterosexism (p. 155)
17.   Abortion (p. 156)

True-False

1.	T	(p. 137)	5.	F	(p. 145)
2.	F	(p. 137)	6.	T	(p. 147)
3.	T	(p. 139)	7.	F	(p. 148)
4.	F	(p. 143)	8.	T	(pp. 154-155)

Multiple Choice

1.	b	(p. 136)	9.	e	(pp. 146-147)
2.	c	(p. 137)	10.	c	(p. 147)
3.	d	(p. 138)	11.	c	(pp. 148-149)
4.	e	(p. 139)	12.	b	(pp. 149-150)
5.	c	(p. 141)	13.	c	(pp. 152-153)
6.	b	(p. 143)	14.	c	(pp. 153-154)
7.	a	(p. 143)	15.	c	(p. 155)
8.	e	(p. 145)			

Matching

1.	h	(p. 136)	5.	g	(p. 144)
2.	d	(p. 137)	6.	f	(p. 148)
3.	a	(p. 138)	7.	e	(p. 155)
4.	c	(p. 144)	8.	b	(p. 155)

Fill-In

1. Secondary (p. 137)
2. intersexual people (p. 138)
3. incest taboo (p. 139)
4. society, biology (p. 144)
5. 9, 4 (p. 145)
6. Homophobia (p. 146)
7. moral, power (p. 147)
8. street walkers (p. 148)

PART VII: IN FOCUS--IMPORTANT ISSUES

• Understanding Sexuality

Differentiate between sex as a *biological issue* and as a *cultural issue*.

- Sexual Attitudes in the United States

    What does the author mean by saying that our cultural orientation toward sexuality has always been *inconsistent*?

    How strong do you believe the *sexual double standard* is in our society today? What is your evidence?

- Sexual Orientation

    How have attitudes toward *homosexuality* changed in our society over the last fifty years? What factors have influenced our society's attitudes toward homosexuality?

- Sexual Controversies

    Identify two major points made in the text concerning each of the following four controversial issues:

        teen pregnancy

        pornography

        prostitution

        sexual violence

- Theoretical Analysis of Sexuality

    According to *structural-functionalists*, why is it important for society to regulate sexuality?

    Provide an illustration of how global comparisons can be used to illustrate the symbolic-interactionists' view that sexuality is *socially constructed*.

    According to social-conflict theorists, how is sexuality involved in the creation and maintenance of *social inequality*?

Chapter 7 | Deviance

PART I: CHAPTER OUTLINE

I. What is Deviance?
- A. The Biological Context
- B. Personality Factors
- C. The Social Foundations of Deviance

II. The Functions of Deviance: Structural-Functional Analysis
- A. Durkheim's Basic Insight
- B. Merton's Strain Theory
- C. Deviant Subcultures

III. Labeling Deviance: Symbolic-Interaction Analysis
- A. Labeling Theory
- B. Primary and Secondary Deviance
- C. Stigma
- D. Labeling Difference as Deviance
- E. The Medicalization of Deviance
- F. Sutherland's Differential Association Theory
- G. Hirschi's Control Theory

IV. Deviance and Inequality: Social Conflict Analysis
- A. Deviance and Power
- B. Deviance and Capitalism
- C. White-Collar Crime
- D. Corporate Crime
- E. Organized Crime

V. Deviance and Social Diversity
- A. Hate Crimes
- B. Deviance and Gender

VI. Crime
- A. Types of Crime
- B. Criminal Statistics
- C. The Street Criminal: A Profile
  - 1. Age
  - 2. Gender
  - 3. Social Class
  - 4. Race and Ethnicity
- D. Crime in Global Perspective

PART II: LEARNING OBJECTIVES

- To explain how deviance is interpreted as a product of society.
- To identify and evaluate the biological explanation of deviance.
- To identify and evaluate the sociological explanations of deviance.
- To compare and contrast different theories representative of the three major sociological approaches.
- To distinguish among the types of crime.
- To become more aware of the demographic patterns of crime in our society.
- To evaluate deviance and crime in global perspective.
- To identify and describe the elements of the American criminal justice system.

PART III: KEY CONCEPTS

1. _____ refers to the recognized violation of cultural norms.

2. _____ refers to the violation of a society's formally enacted criminal law.

3. Attempts by society to regulate people's thought and behavior is known as _____ _____.

4. The _____ _____ _____ refers to a formal response by police, courts, and prison officials to alleged violations of the law.

5. _____ _____ is the assertion that deviance and conformity result not so much from what people do as from how others respond to those actions.

6. A powerfully negative label that greatly changes a person's self-concept and social identity is called a _____.

7. The _____ _____ _____ refers to the transformation of moral and legal deviance into a medical condition.

8. _____ _____ refers to crime committed by people of high social position in the course of their occupations.

9. The illegal actions of a corporation or people acting on its behalf is known as _____ _____.

10. _____ _____ refers to a business supplying illegal goods or services.

11. A criminal act against a person or person's property by an offender motivated by racial or other bias is a _____ _____.

12. _____ _____ _____ _____ are crimes that direct violence or the threat of violence against others.

13. _____ _____ _____ are crimes that involve theft of property belonging to others.

14. Violations of law in which there are no readily apparent victims are called _____ _____.

15. A legal negotiation in which a prosecutor reduces a charge in exchange for a defendant's guilty plea is referred to as _____ _____.

16. _____ is an act of moral vengeance by which society inflicts on the offender suffering comparable to that caused by the offense.

17. The use of punishment to discourage criminality is called _____.

18. _____ is a program for reforming the offender to prevent subsequent offenses.

19. A means by which society renders an offender incapable of further offenses, either temporarily through incarceration or permanently by execution, is called _____ _____.

20. _____ _____ is defined as subsequent offenses by people convicted of crimes.

21. _____ _____ _____ are correctional programs operating within society at large rather than behind prison walls.

PART IV: IMPORTANT RESEARCHERS

In the space provided below each of the following researchers, write two or three sentences to help you remember his or her respective contributions to the field of sociology.

Caesare Lombroso   William Sheldon

Steven Spitzer   Richard Cloward and Lloyd Ohlin

Erving Goffman   Albert Cohen and Walter Miller

Walter Reckless and Simon Dintz   Edwin Sutherland

Thomas Szasz   Emile Durkheim

Robert Merton   Travis Hirschi

PART V: STUDY QUESTIONS

True-False

1.   T   F   Scientific research clearly concludes that there is absolutely no relationship between *biology* and crime.
2.   T   F   One of the *social foundations of deviance* is that deviance exists only in relation to cultural norms.
3.   T   F   Walter Miller's *subcultural theory* of deviance points out that deviant subcultures have *no focal concerns*, and therefore have no social norms to guide the behavior of their members.
4.   T   F   Edwin Sutherland's *differential association theory* suggests that certain individuals are incapable of learning from experience and therefore are more likely to become deviant.
5.   T   F   The *social-conflict* perspective links deviance to social inequality and power in society.
6.   T   F   Almost every society in the world applies more stringent normative controls on *men* than to *women*.
7.   T   F   Using *index crimes*, the crime rate in the United States is relatively high compared to European societies.
8.   T   F   *Plea bargaining* accounts for about forty percent of criminal cases resolved by the courts.

Multiple Choice

1.   _____ refers to the recognized violation of cultural norms.

    (a)   Crime
    (b)   Deviance
    (c)   Residual behavior
    (d)   Social control

2.   *Containment theory* is an example of a(n) _____ explanation of deviance.

    (a)   biological
    (b)   economic
    (c)   anthropological
    (d)   sociological
    (e)   psychological

3.   Emile Durkheim theorized that all but which of the following are *functions of deviance*?

        (a)   It clarifies moral boundaries.
        (b)   It affirms cultural values and norms.
        (c)   It encourages social stability.
        (d)   It promotes social unity.

4.   According to Robert Merton's *strain theory*, one response to the inability to succeed is _____, or the rejection of both cultural goals and means--so one, in effect, "drops out."

        (a)   innovation
        (b)   retreatism
        (c)   inertia
        (d)   ritualism

5.   Which of the following is *not* an example of a *deviant subculture* identified in Richard Cloward and Lloyd Ohlin's research on delinquents.

        (a)   criminal
        (b)   retreatist
        (c)   conflict
        (d)   residual

6.   Which of the following is *not* an appropriate criticism of *structural-functional theories* of deviance?

        (a)   The theories assume a diversity of cultural standards.
        (b)   The theories seem to imply that everyone who breaks the rules is labeled as deviant.
        (c)   The theories seem to focus on, and unfairly target, the lower class.
        (d)   The theories cannot explain very well certain types of crime.

7.   Skipping school for the first time as an eighth grader is an example of

        (a)   recidivism.
        (b)   primary deviance.
        (c)   a degradation ceremony.
        (d)   secondary deviance.

8.   What is Erving Goffman's term for a powerful negative social label that radically changes a person's self-concept and social identity?

        (a)   anomie
        (b)   secondary deviance
        (c)   medicalization of deviance
        (d)   retribution
        (e)   stigma

9.   Once people stigmatize an individual, they may engage in _____ labeling, or interpreting someone's past in light of some present deviance.

(a)   retrospective
(b)   projective
(c)   residual
(d)   ad hoc

10.   The *medicalization of deviance* is the

(a)   recognition of the true source of deviance.
(b)   objective, clinical approach to deviant behavior.
(c)   transformation of moral and legal issues into medical models.
(d)   discovery of the links between biochemical properties and deviance.

11.   *Attachment, involvement, commitment,* and *belief* are all types of social control in _____ theory.

(a)   Sutherland's differential association
(b)   Durkheim's functional
(c)   Goffman's labeling
(d)   Cohen's subcultural
(e)   Hirschi's control

12.   According to the *social-conflict* approach, who and what is labeled deviant is based primarily on

(a)   the severity of the deviant act.
(b)   psychological profile.
(c)   the functions being served.
(d)   which categories of people hold power in society.
(e)   the location of the deviant act.

13.   The statements "While what is deviant may vary, deviance itself is found in all societies"; "Deviance and the social response it provokes serve to maintain the moral foundation of society"; "Deviance can direct social change" all help to summarize which sociological explanation of deviance?

(a)   structural-functional
(b)   social-conflict
(c)   symbolic-interaction
(d)   labeling
(e)   social exchange

14.   Which contribution below is attributed to the *structural-functional theory* of deviance?

(a)   Nothing is inherently deviant.
(b)   Deviance is found in all societies.
(c)   The reactions of others to deviance are highly variable.
(d)   Laws and other norms reflect the interests of the powerful in society.

70

15. Which of the following are included as part of the FBI *index crimes*?

    (a)   white-collar crime and property crime
    (b)   victimless crime and federal crime
    (c)   crime against the state and civil crime
    (d)   crimes against the person and crimes against property
    (e)   violent crime and white-collar crime

Matching

1. _____ Attempts by society to regulate people's thought and behavior.
2. _____ A theory that suggests that a person's tendency toward conformity or deviance depends on the amount of contact with others who encourage or reject conventional behavior.
3. _____ The illegal actions of a corporation or people acting on its behalf.
4. _____ A business supplying illegal goods or services.
5. _____ A legal negotiation in which a prosecutor reduces a charge in exchange for a defendant's guilty plea.
6. _____ The use of punishment to discourage criminality.
7. _____ A program for reforming the offender to prevent subsequent offenses.
8. _____ Subsequent offenses by people convicted of crimes.

a.	differential association theory	e.	social control
b.	rehabilitation	f.	plea bargaining
c.	criminal recidivism	g.	organized crime
d.	corporate crime	h.	deterrence

Fill-In

1. Activity that is initially defined as deviant is called _____ *deviance*. On the other hand, a person who accepts the label of deviant may then engage in _____ *deviance*, or behavior caused by the person's incorporating the deviant label into their self-concept.
2. Psychiatrist Thomas Szasz argues that *mental illness* is a _____.
3. Whether we define deviance as a *moral* or *medical* issue has three consequences. First, it affects who _____ to the deviance. Second, it affects _____ people will respond to deviance. And third, the two labels differ on the personal _____ of the deviant person.
4. Travis Hirschi links *conformity* to four types of social control, including _____, _____, _____, and _____.
5. _____ *crime* is defined as crimes committed by persons of high social position in the course of their occupations.
6. Technically, all crime is composed of two elements: the _____ and the criminal _____.
7. The four basic *justifications for punishment* include: _____, _____, _____, and _____.
8. Subsequent offenses by people previously convicted of crimes is termed *criminal* _____.

<u>Discussion</u>

1. According to Travis Hirschi's *control theory,* there are four types of social controls. What are these?
2. According to Robert Merton's *strain theory*, what are the four deviant responses by individuals to dominant cultural patterns when there is a gap between *means* and *goals*?
3. Describe Thomas Szasz's view of mental illness and deviance. What are your opinions of his arguments?
4. *Social-conflict* theorist Steven Spitzer argues that deviant labels are applied to people who impede the operation of *capitalism*. What are the four reasons he gives for this phenomenon?
5. How do researchers using *differential association theory* explain deviance?
6. What is meant by the term *medicalization of deviance*? Provide two illustrations.
7. According to Elliott Currie, what factors are responsible for the relatively high crime rates in the United States? Critique the official statistics of crime in the United States. What are the weaknesses of the measures used in the identification of *crime rates*?
8. Briefly review the demographic *profile* of the *street criminal*. What are the four *justifications* for the use of punishment against criminals? What evidence exists for their relative effectiveness?

PART VI: ANSWERS TO STUDY QUESTIONS

<u>Key Concepts</u>

1. Deviance (p. 162)
2. Crime (p. 162)
3. social control (p. 163)
4. criminal justice system (p. 163)
5. Labeling theory (p. 167)
6. stigma (p. 168)
7. medicalization of deviance (p. 169)
8. White-collar crime (p. 172)
9. corporate crime (p. 172)
10. Organized crime (p. 172)
11. hate crime (p. 173)
12. Crimes against the person (p. 175)
13. Crimes against property (p. 175)
14. victimless crimes (p. 176)
15. plea bargaining (p. 182)
16. Retribution (p. 182)
17. deterrence (p. 182)
18. Rehabilitation (p. 183)
19. societal protection (p. 183)
20. Criminal recidivism (p. 184)
21. Community-based corrections (p. 185)

<u>True-False</u>

1.	F	(pp. 163-164)	5.	T	(p. 171)
2.	T	(p. 164)	6.	F	(pp. 174-175)

3.	F	(p. 166)		7.	T	(pp. 178-179)
4.	F	(p. 170)		8.	F	(p. 182)

Multiple Choice

1.	b	(p. 162)		9.	a	(p. 169)
2.	e	(p. 164)		10.	c	(p. 169)
3.	c	(p. 165)		11.	e	(p. 170)
4.	b	(pp. 165-166)		12.	d	(p. 171)
5.	d	(p. 166)		13.	a	(p. 173)
6.	a	(p. 167)		14.	b	(p. 173)
7.	b	(pp. 167-168)		15.	d	(pp. 175-176)
8.	e	(pp. 168-169)				

Matching

1.	e	(p. 163)		5.	f	(p. 182)
2.	a	(p. 170)		6.	h	(p. 182)
3.	d	(p. 172)		7.	b	(p. 183)
4.	g	(p. 172)		8.	c	(p. 184)

Fill-In

1. primary, secondary (pp. 167-168)
2. myth (p. 169)
3. responds, how, competence (p. 169)
4. attachment, opportunity, involvement, belief (p. 170)
5. White-collar (p. 172)
6. act, intent (p. 175)
7. retribution, deterrence, rehabilitation, societal protection (pp. 182-183)
8. recidivism (p. 184)

PART VII: IN FOCUS--IMPORTANT ISSUES

- What is Deviance?

    What role does *biology* play in helping us explain deviance?

    Using *containment theory*, how did Walter Reckless and Simon Dinitz explain delinquency among young boys?

- Structural-Functional Analysis

  According to Emile Durkheim, what are the four *functions of deviance*?

  In Robert Merton's *strain theory,* four adaptations to conformity are identified. List, define, and illustrate each of these.

- Symbolic-Interaction Analysis

  How is deviance explained using *labeling theory*?

  What is meant by the *medicalization of deviance*? Provide an illustration of this phenomenon.

  How is deviance explained using Edwin Sutherland's *differential association theory*?

  Using Travis Hirschi's *control theory*, four types of social control are identified. Illustrate each of these.

- Social-Conflict Analysis

  Social-conflict theory explains the relationship between *deviance and power* in three ways. Identify each of these ways.

  Steven Spitzer suggests that deviant labels are applied to people who interfere with the operation of *capitalism*. Identify the four ways he says this is the case.

- Deviance and Social Diversity

    Using the following categories, describe the demographic patterns of *street crime* in our societies.

        age

        gender

        social class

        race and ethnicity

- The Criminal Justice System

    Identify two important points being made by the author about each of the following *components of the criminal justice system.*

        police

        courts

        punishment

Chapter 8 — Social Stratification

PART I: CHAPTER OUTLINE

PART II: LEARNING OBJECTIVES

- To understand the four basic principles of social stratification.
- To differentiate between the caste and class systems of stratification.
- To begin to understand the relationship between ideology and stratification.
- To describe and differentiate between the structural-functional and social-conflict perspectives of stratification.
- To describe the views of Max Weber concerning the dimensions of social class.
- To have a clear sense of the extent of social inequality in the United States.
- To recognize the role of economic resources, power, occupational prestige, and schooling in the class system of the United States.
- To generally describe the various social classes in our social stratification system.
- To begin to develop a sociological sense about the nature of social mobility in the United States.

PART III: KEY CONCEPTS

1. _____ _____ refers to a system by which a society ranks categories of people in a hierarchy.
2. Change in one's position in the social hierarchy is called _____ _____.
3. A _____ _____ refers to social stratification based on ascription, or birth.
4. A _____ _____ refers to social stratification based on both birth and individual achievement.
5. Social stratification based on personal merit is known as a _____.

6. _____ _____ refers to the degree of consistency in a person's social standing across various dimensions of social inequality.

7. _____ _____ _____ refers to a shift in the social position of large numbers of people due more to changes in society itself than to individual efforts.

8. _____ refers to cultural beliefs that justify social stratification.

9. The _____ _____ refers to the assertion that social stratification is a universal pattern because it benefits the operation of society.

10. People who own and operate factories and other businesses in pursuit of profits are called _____.

11. Those that sell their productive labor for wages are _____.

12. _____ refers to the experience of isolation and misery resulting from powerlessness.

13. _____ _____ refer to lower-prestige work that involves mostly manual labor.

14. _____ _____ refer to higher-prestige work that involves mostly mental activity.

15. _____ _____ (SES) refers to a composite ranking based on various dimensions of social inequality.

16. _____ refers to wages or salary from work and earnings from investments.

17. _____ refers to the total value of money and other assets, minus outstanding debts.

18. _____ _____ _____ refers to a change in social position occurring during a person's lifetime.

19. _____ _____ _____ refers to upward or downward social mobility of children in relation to their parents.

20. The deprivation of some people in relation to those who have more is known as _____ _____.

21. A deprivation of resources that is life threatening is referred to as _____ _____.

22. The _____ ___ _____ refers to the trend by which women represent an increasing proportion of the poor.

PART IV: IMPORTANT RESEARCHERS

In the space provided below each of the following researchers, write two or three sentences to help you remember his or her respective contributions to the field of sociology.

Karl Marx   Max Weber

Gerhard and Jean Lenski   Kingsley Davis and Wilbert Moore

Ralf Dahrendorf   Melvin Tumin

William Julius Wilson   Oscar Lewis

Max Weber

PART V: STUDY QUESTIONS

True-False

1.   T   F   *Ascription* is fundamental to social-stratification systems based on *castes*.
2.   T   F   A *meritocracy* is a social stratification system based on birth and other ascribed statuses.
3.   T   F   Karl Marx's social conflict theory of social stratification identified two basic relationships to the means of production--those who own productive property, and those who labor for others.
4.   T   F   Sociologist Max Weber developed a unidimensional model of social stratification that was dominant in the early part of the twentieth century.
5.   T   F   When financial assets are balanced against debits, the lowest-ranking 40 percent of families in the U.S. have virtually no wealth at all.
6.   T   F   Cultural values vary by social class. *Affluent* people with greater education and financial security are more tolerant of controversial behavior such as homosexuality.
7.   T   F   *Intragenerational social mobility* refers to a change in social position occurring during a person's lifetime.
8.   T   F   The concept *culture of poverty* is a term relating poverty to a lower-class subculture that inhibits personal achievement and fosters resignation.

Multiple Choice

1. What is a *caste system*?

   (a)   social stratification based on ascription
   (b)   social stratification based on meritocracy
   (c)   social stratification based on achievement
   (d)   any system in which there is social inequality

2. Which of the following is *not* one of the four *castes* in India's traditional caste system?

   (a)   Vaishya
   (b)   Jaishra
   (c)   Shudra
   (d)   Brahmin
   (e)   Kshatriya

3. In the Middle Ages, social stratification in England was a system of three

   (a)   open classes.
   (b)   absolute castes.
   (c)   meritocracies.
   (d)   closed classes.
   (e)   caste-like estates.

4. What do sociologists call a shift in the social position of large numbers of people due more to changes in society itself than to individual efforts?

(a) perestroika
(b) bureaucratization
(c) linear social stratification
(d) structural social mobility

5. What is *ideology*?

(a) a system in which entire categories of people are ranked in a hierarchy
(b) ideas that are generated through scientific investigation
(c) views and opinions that are based on the principle of cultural relativism
(d) ideas that limit the amount of inequality of a society
(e) cultural beliefs that serve to justify social stratification

6. The *Davis-Moore thesis* asserts that

(a) social stratification has beneficial consequences for the operation of society.
(b) industrialization produces greater, and more harmful social stratification than previous forms of subsistence.
(c) social stratification based on meritocracy has dysfunctional consequences for society and its individual members.
(d) ideology undermines social stratification.
(e) industrial capitalism is moving toward a classless social order.

7. In Karl Marx's analysis of social stratification, another name for the working class is the

(a) primogeniture.
(b) perestroika.
(c) apparatchiks.
(d) proletariat.
(e) bourgeoisie.

8. Which of the following is *not* one of the dimensions of social stratification according to Max Weber?

(a) class
(b) education
(c) power
(d) status

9. Census Bureau data show that *income* and *wealth* are unequally distributed in the United States. Which of the following statements is most accurate?

    (a) The median family income in the United States in 2002 was $68,036.
    (b) The top five percent of households (by income) receive 65 percent of the income earned in the United States.
    (c) The poorest 20 percent of households receive about 10 percent of the income earned in the United States.
    (d) Wealth is distributed more unequally in the United States than is income.

10. Recent government calculations put the *wealth* of the average U.S. household at about

    (a) $10,000.
    (b) $25,000.
    (c) $38,000.
    (d) $50,000.
    (e) $71,600.

11. The *median* wealth for minority families, including African Americans, Hispanics, and Asians (about $17,100), is just _____ percent of the median for non-Hispanic white households.

    (a) 50
    (b) 8
    (c) 65
    (d) 14

12. The *middle class* includes approximately what percentage of the U.S. population?

    (a) 20-25
    (b) 40-45
    (c) 30-35
    (d) 55-60

13. A change in social position of children relative to that of their parents is called

    (a) horizontal social mobility.
    (b) structural social mobility.
    (c) intergenerational social mobility.
    (d) intragenerational social mobility.

14. For a family of four, the 2002 poverty line was set at

    (a) $18,392.
    (b) $9,453.
    (c) $26,068.
    (d) $12,892.

15.   The *culture of poverty* view concerning the causes of poverty

    (a)   holds that the poor are primarily responsible for their own poverty.
    (b)   blames poverty on economic stagnation relating to the globalization of the U.S. economy.
    (c)   sees lack of ambition on the part of the poor as a consequence, not a cause, for poverty.
    (d)   views the conservative economic policies of the last two decades in the U.S. as the primary reason for relatively high poverty rates.

Matching

1. ____   The total value of money and other assets, minus outstanding debts.
2. ____   Encompasses 40 to 45 percent of the U.S. population and exerts a tremendous influence on U.S. culture.
3. ____   Accounts for about one-third of the U.S. population.
4. ____   A change in social position occurring within a person's lifetime.
5. ____   Upward or downward social mobility of children in relation to their parents.
6. ____   Describes the trend by which women represent an increasing proportion of the poor.
7. ____   Developed the concept of the *culture of poverty*, or a lower-class subculture that inhibits personal achievement and fosters resignation to one's plight.
8. ____   Argued that *society* is primarily responsible for poverty and that any lack of ambition on the part of the poor is a *consequence* of insufficient opportunity.

    a. William Julius Wilson   e. intragenerational social mobility
    b. intergenerational social mobility f. the working-class
    c. feminization of poverty   g. Oscar Lewis
    d. wealth   h. the middle-class

Fill-In

1. Social stratification is a matter of four *basic principles*: it is a characteristic of _____, not simply a reflection of individual differences; it _____ over generations; it is _____ but variable; and it involves not just inequality but _____.
2. _____ refers to cultural beliefs that justify social stratification.
3. Four reasons listed in the text as to why there has been *no Marxist revolution* include the _____ of the capitalist class, a _____ standard of living, more extensive worker _____, and more extensive legal _____.
4. The *Kuznets curve* shows that greater _____ sophistication is generally accompanied by more pronounced social stratification.
5. When financial assets are balanced against debts, the lowest-ranking _____ percent of U.S. families have virtually no *wealth* at all.
6. Much of the disparity in income between whites and African Americans is due to the larger share of single-parent families among African Americans. Comparing only families headed by *married couples*, African Americans earn _____ percent as much as non-Hispanic whites.
7. While the relationship between social class and politics is complex, generally, members of high social standing tend to have _____ *views on economic issues* and _____ *views on social issues*.
8. Evidence of "income stagnation" in the United States today includes: for many workers, earnings have _____, _____ job-holding is up, more jobs offer little _____, and young people are remaining _____.

Discussion

1. What are the four *fundamental principles* of social stratification?
2. What are the basic qualities of a *caste system*?
3. Define Karl Marx's concepts of *proletariat* and *capitalists*. What value does Marx's perspective offer to the understanding of modern social stratification?
4. Provide an illustration of *structural social mobility* in our society.
5. What are some of the reasons why people in the United States might tend to underestimate the extent of social inequality in our society?
6. Using the factors of health, values, and politics, discuss the difference social class makes in the lives of people within our society.
7. What are the four general conclusions being made about *social mobility* in the United States today?
8. What is the evidence that the *American Dream* is waning in our society?

PART VI: ANSWERS TO STUDY QUESTIONS

Key Concepts

1. Social stratification (p. 192)
2. social mobility (p. 192)
3. caste system (p. 193)
4. class system (p. 195)
5. meritocracy (p. 195)
6. Status consistency (p. 195)
7. Structural social mobility (p. 197)
8. Ideology (p. 198)
9. Davis-Moore thesis (p. 199)
10. capitalists (p. 200)
11. proletarians (p. 200)
12. Alienation (p. 200)
13. Blue-collar occupations (p. 201)
14. White-collar occupations (p. 201)
15. Socioeconomic status (SES) (p. 202)
16. Income (p. 205)
17. Wealth (pp. 205-206)
18. Intragenerational social mobility (p. 211)
19. Intergenerational social mobility (p. 211)
20. relative poverty (pp. 215-216)
21. absolute poverty (p. 216)
22. feminization of poverty (p. 217)

True-False

1.	T	(p. 193)	5.	T	(pp. 205-206)
2.	F	(p. 195)	6.	T	(p. 210)
3.	T	(p. 200)	7.	T	(p. 211)
4.	F	(p. 202)	8.	T	(p. 217)

Multiple Choice

1.	a	(p. 193)	9.	d	(pp. 205-206)
2.	b	(p. 193)	10.	e	(p. 206)
3.	e	(p. 195)	11.	d	(p. 208)
4.	d	(p. 197)	12.	b	(p. 209)
5.	e	(p. 198)	13.	c	(p. 211)
6.	a	(p. 199)	14.	a	(p. 216)
7.	d	(p. 200)	15.	a	(p. 217)
8.	b	(p. 202)			

Matching

1.	d	(pp. 205-206)	5.	b	(p. 211)
2.	h	(p. 209)	6.	c	(p. 217)
3.	f	(p. 209)	7.	g	(p. 217)
4.	e	(p. 211)	8.	a	(pp. 217-218)

Fill-In

1. society, persists, universal, beliefs (pp. 192-193)
2. Ideology (p. 198)
3. fragmentation, higher, organizations, protections (p. 201)
4. technological (p. 203)
5. 40 (p. 206)
6. 80 (p. 206)
7. conservative, liberal (p. 208)
8. stalled, multiple, income, home (p. 213)

PART VII: IN FOCUS—IMPORTANT ISSUES

• What is Social Stratification?

What are the four basic *principles of social stratification*?

• Caste and Class Systems

Identify three major characteristics of a *caste system*.

Identify three major characteristics of a *class system*.

- Stratification and Conflict

    What was Karl Marx's argument about *class and conflict*?

    Define each of the three *dimensions of social stratification* as identified by Max Weber.

- Stratification and Technology: A Global Perspective

    According to the *Kuznets curve*, describe the relationship between technology and social stratification throughout history:

- Inequality in the United States

    Our author suggests that U.S. society is *highly stratified*. What are two pieces of evidence that support this view?

    Briefly discuss how each of the following variables impact social stratification in the United States.

        income, wealth, and power

        occupational prestige

        schooling

        ancestry, race, and gender

- Social Classes in the United States

    Briefly describe the major social class divisions in the United States.

- The Difference Class Makes

    Social stratification affects many dimensions of our lives. How are each of the following connected to social class?

        health

        values and attitudes

        family and gender

- Social Mobility

    What are the four *general conclusions* being made in the text concerning social mobility in the United States?

- Poverty in the United States

    Describe the *demographics of poverty* using the following variables:

        age

        race and ethnicity

        gender and family patterns

        urban and rural poverty

    Briefly summarize the following two *explanations of poverty*.

        blame the poor

        blame society

<table>
<tr><td>Chapter

9</td><td># Global
Stratification</td></tr>
</table>

PART I: CHAPTER OUTLINE

PART II: LEARNING OBJECTIVES

- To define global stratification and describe the demographics of the three "economic development" categories used to classify nations of the world.

- To begin to understand both the severity and extensiveness of poverty in the low-income nations of the world.
- To recognize the extent to which women are overrepresented among the poor of the world and the factors leading to this condition.
- To identify and describe the stages of modernization.
- To recognize the problems facing women as a result of modernization in the low-income nations of the world.
- To identify the keys to combating global inequality over the next century.

PART III: KEY CONCEPTS

1. _____ _____ refers to patterns of social inequality in the world as a whole.
2. _____ _____ _____ are the richest nations with the highest overall standards of living.
3. _____ _____ _____ are nations with a standard of living about average for the world as a whole.
4. _____ _____ _____ are nations with a low standard of living in which most people are poor.
5. _____ refers to the process by which some nations enrich themselves through political and economic control of other nations.
6. _____ is a new form of global power relationships that involves not direct political control but economic exploitation by multinational corporations.
7. A large business that operates in many countries is known as a _____ _____.
8. _____ _____ is a model of economic and social development that explains global inequality in terms of technological and cultural differences between societies.
9. _____ _____ is a model of economic and social development that explains global inequality in terms of the historical exploitation of poor societies by rich ones.

PART IV: IMPORTANT RESEARCHERS

In the space provided below each of the following researchers, write two or three sentences to help you remember his respective contributions to sociology.

Immanuel Wallerstein   W. W. Rostow

PART V: STUDY QUESTIONS

True-False

1.   T   F   Global income is so concentrated, even people in the United States with incomes *below the government's poverty line* live far better than the majority of the earth's people.

2.	T	F	The richest 20 percent of the global population receives about 50 percent of all the *income*.
3.	T	F	*High-income countries*, representing about 18 percent of humanity, control over one-half of the world's income.
4.	T	F	Approximately 50 percent of the world's population live in *low-income countries*.
5.	T	F	The United States has the highest *quality of life score* in the world.
6.	T	F	*Modernization theory* suggests the greatest barrier to economic development is *tradition*.
7.	T	F	Immanuel Wallerstein's capitalist world economy model is used to illustrate and support *dependency theory*.
8.	T	F	As low-income countries increase the standard of living for their citizens, *stress* on the *physical environment* is expected to be reduced.

Multiple Choice

1. The poorest 20 percent of the world's nations controls _____ percent of the *global income*.

   (a) 12
   (b) 10
   (c) 15
   (d) 1
   (e) 5

2. The *high-income countries*, representing 18 percent of the world's population, control over _____ percent of the world's income.

   (a) 25
   (b) 35
   (c) 50
   (d) 80

3. Which of the following statements concerning the *high-income countries* is/are accurate?

   (a) Taken together, countries with the most developed economies cover roughly 25 percent of the earth's land area.
   (b) About three-fourths of the people in high-income countries live in or near cities.
   (c) Significant cultural differences exist among high-income countries.
   (d) Production in rich nations is capital-intensive.
   (e) All of the above are accurate statements.

4. Which of the following is an *inaccurate* statement concerning *middle-income countries*?

   (a) In middle-income countries, per capita income ranges between $2,500 and $10,000.
   (b) About one-third of the people in middle-income countries still live in rural areas.
   (c) One cluster of middle-income countries includes the former Soviet Union and the nations of Eastern Europe.
   (d) Taken together, middle-income countries span roughly 65 percent of the earth's land area.

5. *Middle-income countries* cover _____ percent of the earth's land area and contain slightly more than _____ percent of humanity.

    (a) 55; 70
    (b) 30; 80
    (c) 25; 15
    (d) 10; 25
    (e) 65; 30

6. What percentage of the world's population lives in the *low-income countries* of the world?

    (a) 52
    (b) 12
    (c) 77
    (d) 85
    (e) 95

7. Which of the following is an *accurate* statement regarding poverty and women?

    (a) In rich societies, the work that women do tends to be undervalued, underpaid, or overlooked entirely.
    (b) In poor societies, women's work is highly valued.
    (c) Women in poor countries generally have adequate access to birth control.
    (d) About 20 percent of the world's 1 billion people living hear absolute poverty are women.

8. Which of the following is *not* a type of *slavery* identified in the text?

    (a) chattel
    (b) child
    (c) colonial
    (d) servile forms of marriage
    (e) debt bondage

9. Which of the following is *not* discussed as a correlate of *global poverty*?

    (a) gender inequality
    (b) population growth
    (c) technology
    (d) social stratification
    (e) all are discussed

10.   *Neocolonialism* is

  (a)   primarily an overt political force.
  (b)   a form of economic exploitation that does not involve formal political control.
  (c)   the economic power of the low-income countries being used to control the consumption patterns in the high-income countries.
  (d)   the exploitation of the high-income countries by the low-income countries.

11.   A model of economic and social development that explains global inequality in terms of technological and cultural differences among societies is _____ theory.

  (a)   colonial
  (b)   dependency
  (c)   modernization
  (d)   ecological

12.   *Modernization theory* identifies _____ as the greatest barrier to economic development.

  (a)   technology
  (b)   social equality
  (c)   social power
  (d)   tradition

13.   Which of the following is *not* a criticism of modernization theory?

  (a)   It tends to minimize the connection between rich and poor societies.
  (b)   It tends to blame the low-income countries for their own poverty.
  (c)   It ignores historical facts that thwart development in poor countries.
  (d)   It has held up the world's most developed countries as the standard for judging the rest of humanity.
  (e)   All are criticisms of this theory.

14.   _____ *theory* is a model of economic and social development that explains global inequality in terms of the historical exploitation of poor societies by rich ones.

  (a)   Modernization
  (b)   Colonial
  (c)   Dependency
  (d)   Evolutionary
  (e)   Ecological

15. Which of the following is an *inaccurate* statement regarding *global stratification*?

   (a)   According to the United Nations, one-third of the world's countries are living better than they were in the past.
   (b)   One insight, offered by modernization theory, is that poverty is partly a problem of technology.
   (c)   One insight, derived from dependency theory, is that global inequality is also a political issue.
   (d)   While economic development increases living standards, it also establishes a context for less strain being placed on the environment.

Matching

1. ___   Percentage of the world's income controlled by the poorest fifth of the world's population.
2. ___   Two high-income countries.
3. ___   Two middle-income countries.
4. ___   The percentage of the world's population living in low-income countries.
5. ___   A new form of global power relationships that involves not direct political control but economic exploitation by multinational corporations.
6. ___   The process by which some nations enrich themselves through political and economic control of other nations.
7. ___   Huge businesses that operate in many countries.
8. ___   A model of economic and social development that explains global inequality in terms of technological and cultural differences among societies.

   a.   Chile and Malaysia   e.   1
   b.   modernization theory   f.   12
   c.   multinational corporations   g.   Canada and Singapore
   d.   colonialism   h.   neocolonialism

Fill-In

1. According to the author, compared to the older "three worlds" model, the new classification system used in the text has two main advantages, including a focus on the single most important dimension that underlies social life--_____ _____.

2. The *correlates of global poverty* include: _____, population _____, _____ patterns, social _____, _____ inequality, and global _____ relationships.

3. _____ is a new form of economic exploitation that does not involve formal political control.

4. W. W. Rostow's stages of modernization include: the _____, _____, drive to _____ maturity, and high mass _____.

5. _____ *theory* maintains that global poverty historically stems from the exploitation of poor societies by rich societies.

6. *Modernization theory* maintains that rich societies _____ _____ through capital investment and technological innovation.

7. *Dependency theory* claims that the world economy makes poor nations dependent on rich ones. This dependency involves three factors: narrow, _____ *economies*, lack of _____ *capacity*, and _____ *debt*.

8. Two keys to combating global inequality during this century will be seeing it partly as a problem of _____ and that it is also a _____ issue.

Discussion

1. Define the terms *high-income, middle-income,* and *low-income countries*. Identify the key characteristics of each category. Does this resolve the "terminology" problem?
2. What factors create the condition of *women* being overrepresented in poverty around the world?
3. What are the *correlates* of global poverty? Describe each.
4. What is *neocolonialism*? Provide an illustration.
5. What are the four stages of *modernization* in Rostow's model of societal change and development?
6. What are the *problems* faced by women in poor countries as a result of modernization?
7. According to *modernization* theorists, in what respects are rich nations part of the solution to global poverty?
8. Differentiate between how *modernization theory* and *dependency theory* view the primary causes of global inequality. Critique each of these theories, identifying the strengths and weaknesses of each in terms of explaining global poverty. How do each differ in terms of recommendations to improve the conditions in low-income countries?

PART VI: ANSWERS TO STUDY QUESTIONS

Key Concepts

1. Global stratification (p. 226)
2. High-income countries (p. 227)
3. Middle-income countries (p. 227)
4. Low-income countries (p. 227)
5. Colonialism (p. 238)
6. Neocolonialism (p. 238)
7. multinational corporation (p. 238)
8. Modernization theory (p. 238)
9. Dependency theory (p. 241)

True-False

1.	T	(p. 227)	5.	F	(p. 232)
2.	F	(p. 227)	6.	T	(p. 238)
3.	T	(p. 228)	7.	T	(p. 242)
4.	F	(p. 229)	8.	F	(p. 247)

Multiple Choice

1.	d	(p. 227)	9.	e	(pp. 236-238)
2.	c	(p. 228)	10.	b	(p. 238)
3.	e	(pp. 228-229)	11.	c	(p. 238)
4.	d	(p. 229)	12.	d	(p. 238)
5.	a	(p. 229)	13.	e	(pp. 240-241)
6.	b	(p. 229)	14.	c	(p. 241)
7.	a	(p. 234)	15.	d	(pp. 244-246)
8.	c	(pp. 235-236)			

Matching

1.	e	(p. 227)	5.	h	(p. 238)
2.	g	(p. 228)	6.	d	(p. 238)
3.	a	(p. 229)	7.	c	(p. 238)
4.	f	(p. 229)	8.	b	(p. 238)

Fill-In

1. economic development (p. 227)
2. technology, growth, cultural, stratification, gender, power (pp. 236-238)
3. Neocolonialism (p. 238)
4. traditional, take-off, technological, consumption (pp. 238-239)
5. Dependency (p. 241)
6. produce wealth (p. 240)
7. export-oriented, industrial, foreign (p. 242)
8. technology, political (p. 246)

PART VII: IN FOCUS—IMPORTANT ISSUES

- Global Stratification

    Describe the general characteristics for each of the following categories of countries.

        high-income countries

        middle-income countries

        low-income countries

Describe how each of the following are *correlates of poverty*.

>technology

>population growth

>cultural patterns

>social stratification

>gender inequality

>global power relationships

- Global Stratification: Theoretical Analysis

What are the major tenets of *modernization theory*?

Outline and describe *Rostow's stages of modernization*.

What are the basic tenets of *dependency theory*?

According to Immanuel Wallerstein, what are the three factors involved in the dependency of poor nations on rich nations?

- Global Stratification: Looking Ahead

What is the evidence that global stratification is both an issue of *technology* and *politics*?

Gender Stratification

PART I: CHAPTER OUTLINE

I. Gender and Inequality
    A.   Male-Female Differences
    B.   Gender in Global Perspective
        1.   The Israeli Kibbutzim
        2.   Margaret Mead's Research
        3.   George Murdock's Research
        4.   In Sum: Gender and Culture
    C.   Patriarchy and Sexism
        1.   The Cost of Sexism
        2.   Is Patriarchy Inevitable?

II. Gender and Socialization
    A.   Gender and the Family
    B.   Gender and the Peer Group
    C.   Gender and Schooling
    D.   Gender and the Mass Media

III. Gender and Social Stratification
    A.   Working Women and Men
        1.   Gender and Occupations
    B.   Housework: Women's "Second Shift"
    C.   Gender, Income, and Wealth
    D.   Gender and Education
    E.   Gender and Politics
    F.   Gender and the Military
    G.   Are Women a Minority?
    H.   Minority Women: Intersection Theory
    I.   Violence Against Women
        1.   Sexual Harassment
        2.   Pornography

IV. Theoretical Analysis of Gender
    A.   Structural-Functional Analysis
        1.   Talcott Parsons: Gender and Complementarity
    B.   Social-Conflict Analysis
        1.   Friedrich Engels: Gender and Class

PART II: LEARNING OBJECTIVES

- To know the distinction between male-female differences and gender stratification.
- To become aware of the various types of social organizations found globally based on the relationship between females and males.
- To describe the link between patriarchy and sexism, and to see how the nature of each is changing in modern society.
- To describe the role that gender plays in socialization in the family, the peer group, schooling, the mass media, and adult interaction.
- To see how gender stratification occurs in the work world, education, and politics.
- To consider how the structural-functional and social-conflict approaches help explain the origins and persistence of gender inequality.
- To begin to recognize the extent to which women are victims of violence, and to begin to understand what we can do to change this problem.

PART III: KEY CONCEPTS

1. _____ refers to the personal traits and social positions that members of a society attach to being female and male.
2. _____ _____ refers to the unequal distribution of wealth, power, and privilege between men and women.
3. _____ is a form of social organization in which males dominate females.
4. _____ is a form of social organization in which females dominate males.
5. _____ refers to the belief that one sex is innately superior to the other.
6. Attitudes and activities that a society links to each sex refers to _____ _____.
7. A _____ refers to any category of people, distinguished by physical or cultural difference, that a society sets apart and subordinates.
8. The investigation of the interplay of race, class, and gender, often resulting in multiple dimensions of disadvantage, is called _____ _____.
9. _____ _____ refers to comments, gestures, or physical contact of a sexual nature that are deliberate, repeated, and unwelcome.
10. _____ refers to the advocacy of social equality for men and women, in opposition to patriarchy and sexism.

PART IV: IMPORTANT RESEARCHERS

In the space provided below each of the following researchers, write two or three sentences to help you remember his or her respective contributions to sociology.

Margaret Mead   George Murdock

Talcott Parsons   Janet Lever

Friedrich Engels

PART V: STUDY QUESTIONS

<u>True-False</u>

1.	T	F	*Gender* refers to the biological distinction between females and males.
2.	T	F	The experience of the *Israeli Kibbutzim* suggests that cultures have considerable latitude in defining what is masculine and feminine.
3.	T	F	The conclusions made by *Margaret Mead* in her research on three New Guinea societies is consistent with the sociobiological argument that "persistent biological distinctions may undermine gender equality."
4.	T	F	*George Murdock's* cross-cultural research has shown some general patterns in terms of which type of activities are classified as *masculine* or *feminine;* however, beyond this general pattern, significant variation exists.
5.	T	F	Women with children under the age of six years have only about half the proportion of their number working in the labor force as do married women with older children.
6.	T	F	Approximately two-thirds of the *pay gap* between men and women is the result of two factors--types of work and family responsibilities.
7.	T	F	According to the definition given in the text, *sexual harassment* always involves physical contact.
8.	T	F	For structural-functionalists like Talcott Parsons, gender, at least in the traditional sense, forms a *complementary* set of roles that links men and women together.

<u>Multiple Choice</u>

1.   The personal traits and social positions that members of a society attach to being female and male refers to

    (a)   gender.
    (b)   sex.
    (c)   sexual orientation.
    (d)   gender stratification.

2.	The unequal distribution of wealth, power, and privilege between men and women refers to

(a)	secondary sex characteristics.
(b)	gender division.
(c)	gender stratification.
(d)	gender discrimination.

3.	Investigations of the *Israeli Kibbutzim* have indicated

(a)	they are collective settlements.
(b)	their members historically have embraced social equality.
(c)	they support evidence of wide cultural latitude in defining what is feminine and masculine.
(d)	men and women living there share both work and decision making.
(e)	all of the above

4.	Which of the following studies illustrate a connection between *culture* and *gender*?

(a)	Murdock's cross-culture research
(b)	Mead's research in New Guinea
(c)	the Israeli Kibbutz research
(d)	all of the above
(e)	none of the above

5.	Margaret Mead's research on gender in three societies in New Guinea illustrates that

(a)	diffusion tends to standardize gender role assignments for women and men.
(b)	gender is primarily biologically determined.
(c)	gender is treated virtually the same across societies.
(d)	gender is a variable creation of culture.
(e)	while gender roles vary cross-culturally for men, they are very consistent for women.

6.	A form of social organization in which females are dominated by males is termed

(a)	matriarchal.
(b)	oligarchal.
(c)	patriarchy.
(d)	egalitarian.

7.	_____ is/are attitudes and activities that a society links to each sex.

(a)	Gender roles
(b)	Sexual orientation
(c)	Gender stratification
(d)	Gender identity

8.   Research by Carol Gilligan and Janet Lever demonstrates the influence of _____ on gender roles.

    (a)   the peer group
    (b)   biology
    (c)   religion
    (d)   personality

9.   What percentage of *married couples* in the U.S. today depend on two incomes?

    (a)   25
    (b)   59
    (c)   87
    (d)   36

10.   Two-thirds of the *earnings disparity* between men and women is explained by the two variables

    (a)   age and geography.
    (b)   marital status and education.
    (c)   type of work and family responsibilities.
    (d)   father's occupation and health.

11.   As a woman, where are you most likely to suffer *physical violence*?

    (a)   at work
    (b)   at home
    (c)   among friends
    (d)   on the streets

12.   Many feminists want our society to use a(n) _____ standard when measuring for *sexual harassment*.

    (a)   effect
    (b)   intention
    (c)   quid pro quo
    (d)   quid pro quid

13.   *Talcott Parsons* argued that there exist two *complementary role sets* that exist to link males and females together with social institutions. He called these

    (a)   rational and irrational.
    (b)   effective and affective.
    (c)   fundamental and secondary.
    (d)   residual and basic.
    (e)   instrumental and expressive.

14. Which theorist suggested that the male dominance over women was linked to technological advances that led to surpluses of valued resources?

    (a) Talcott Parsons
    (b) Erving Goffman
    (c) Friedrich Engels
    (d) Janet Lever

15. Which of the following is *not* a type of *feminism*?

    (a) liberal
    (b) socialist
    (c) radical
    (d) expressive

Matching

1. ____ The personal traits and social positions that members of a society attach to being female and male.
2. ____ The unequal distribution of wealth, power, and privilege between men and women.
3. ____ Did groundbreaking research on gender in New Guinea.
4. ____ A form of social organization in which females dominate males.
5. ____ The belief that one sex is innately superior to the other.
6. ____ After spending a year watching children at play, concluded that boys favor team sports with complex rules and clear objectives.
7. ____ Any category of people, distinguished by physical or cultural difference, that is socially disadvantaged.
8. ____ The advocacy of social equality for the men and women in opposition to patriarchy and sexism.

    a. matriarchy   e. gender stratification
    b. feminism   f. gender
    c. sexism   g. Margaret Mead
    d. Janet Lever   h. a minority

Fill-In

1. According to research cited in the text, adolescent males exhibit greater _____ ability, while adolescent females excel in _____ skills.
2. Today in the United States, _____ percent of *married women with children under the age of six* are in the labor force.
3. With women's entry into the labor force, the amount of *housework* performed by women has declined, but the _____ women do has stayed about the same.
4. Two factors--type of _____ and _____ responsibilities--account for about two-thirds of the earnings disparities between women and men.
5. A _____ is any category of people, distinguished by physical or cultural difference, that is socially disadvantaged.

6. Traditionally in our society, *pornography* has been viewed as a _____ issue. But, pornography also plays a role in gender stratification and so must also be understood as a _____ issue.

7. Talcott Parsons identified two *complementary roles* that link men and women. These include the _____ and _____.

8. _____ refers to the advocacy of social equality for men and women, in opposition to patriarchy and sexism.

Discussion

1. Compare the research by Margaret Mead in New Guinea with the research done at the Israeli *Kibbutzim* in terms of the cultural variability of gender roles. What generalizations about the linkage between *sex* and *gender* can be made based on the cross-cultural research of George Murdock?

2. According to the author, is *patriarchy* inevitable? Why? What roles have technological advances and industrialization played in the changes in the relative statuses of women and men in society?

3. Identify five important points about *gender stratification* within the occupational domain of our society.
    What evidence can you provide from your own experience and observations concerning the argument being made by Jessie Bernard about the *pink* and *blue* worlds? Do you think her points help you understand how the socialization process creates a context for social inequality between the sexes?

4. What are the explanations as to why males dominate *politics*? To what extent are the roles of women changing in this sphere of social life? What factors are influencing these changes?

5. Review the issue of *violence against women* in our society. What are the types of violence discussed? What are the demographics of violence?

6. Are women a *minority group*? What are the arguments for and against this idea?

7. Compare the analyses of gender stratification as provided through the *structural-functional* and *social-conflict* approaches. What are three general criticisms of the conclusions being made by *social-conflict* theorists and *structural-functionalists* concerning gender stratification?

8. What are the five *basic principles* of *feminism*? Discuss the specific examples for each. What are the three types of *feminism*? Briefly differentiate between them in terms of the basic arguments being made about gender roles in society.

PART VI: ANSWERS TO STUDY QUESTIONS

Key Concepts

1. Gender (p. 252)
2. Gender stratification (p. 252)
3. Patriarchy (p. 254)
4. Matriarchy (p. 254)
5. Sexism (p. 254)
6. gender roles (p. 256)
7. minority (p. 264)
8. intersection theory (p. 265)
9. Sexual harassment (p. 265)
10. Feminism (p. 270)

True-False

1.	F	(p. 252)	5.	F	(p. 259)
2.	T	(p. 253)	6.	T	(pp. 261-262)
3.	F	(pp. 253-254)	7.	F	(p. 265)
4.	T	(p. 254)	8.	T	(pp. 268-269)

Multiple Choice

1.	a	(p. 252)	9.	b	(p. 258)
2.	c	(p. 252)	10.	c	(pp. 261-262)
3.	e	(p. 253)	11.	b	(p. 265)
4.	d	(pp. 253-254)	12.	a	(p. 266)
5.	d	(pp. 253-254)	13.	e	(pp. 268-269)
6.	c	(p. 254)	14.	c	(pp. 269-270)
7.	a	(p. 256)	15.	b	(p. 271)
8.	a	(p. 257)			

Matching

1.	f	(p. 252)	5.	c	(p. 254)
2.	e	(p. 252)	6.	d	(p. 257)
3.	g	(p. 253)	7.	h	(p. 264)
4.	a	(p. 254)	8.	b	(p. 270)

Fill-In

1. mathematical, verbal (p. 253)
2. 63 (p. 259)
3. share (p. 261)
4. work, family (p. 262)
5. minority (p. 264)
6. moral, power (pp. 267-268)
7. instrumental, expressive (p. 269)
8. Feminism (p. 270)

PART VII: IN FOCUS--IMPORTANT ISSUES

- Gender and Inequality

What are the significant biological differences between females and males?

What are three *costs of sexism*?

- Gender and Socialization

    Provide one illustration from the text concerning each of the following influences on *gender role socialization*.

        the family

        the peer group

        schooling

        the mass media

- Gender and Social Stratification

    How does employment status affect women's *housework* labor? How about marital status? The presence of children? What about for men?

    Are women a *minority group*? Why?

    How is *sexual harassment* defined?

    How is *pornography* defined?

- Theoretical Analysis of Gender

    Briefly discuss how each of the following theoretical paradigms views the issue of gender in society:

        structural-functionalism

        social-conflict

- Feminism

    Describe each of the following *types of feminism.*

        liberal

        socialist

        radical

- Looking Ahead: Gender in the Twenty-First Century

    What is the vision offered by the author concerning the role of gender in society over the next century?

<table>
<tr><td>Chapter

11</td><td></td></tr>
</table>

Chapter 11 | Race and Ethnicity

PART I: CHAPTER OUTLINE

I. The Social Meaning of Race and Ethnicity
    A.   Race
        1.   Racial Types
        2.   A Trend toward Mixture
    B.   Ethnicity
    C.   Minorities
    D.   Prejudice and Stereotypes
    E.   Measuring Prejudice: The Social Distance Scale
    F.   Racism
    G.   Theories of Prejudice
        1.   Scapegoat Theory
        2.   Authoritarian Personality Theory
        3.   Culture Theory
        4.   Conflict Theory
    H.   Discrimination
    I.   Institutional Prejudice and Discrimination
    J.   Prejudice and Discrimination: The Vicious Circle
II. Majority and Minority: Patterns of Interaction
    A.   Pluralism
    B.   Assimilation
    C.   Segregation
    D.   Genocide
III. Race and Ethnicity in the United States
    A.   Native Americans
    B.   White Anglo-Saxon Protestants
    C.   African Americans
    D.   Asian Americans
        1.   Chinese Americans
        2.   Japanese Americans
        3.   Recent Asian Immigrants
    E.   Hispanic Americans
        1.   Mexican Americans
        2.   Puerto Ricans
        3.   Cuban Americans

PART II: LEARNING OBJECTIVES

- To develop an understanding about the biological basis for definitions of race.
- To distinguish between the biological concept of race and the cultural concept of ethnicity.
- To identify the characteristics of a minority group.
- To identify and describe the two forms of prejudice.
- To be familiar with the measurement of prejudice using the Social Distance Scale.
- To identify and describe the four theories of prejudice.
- To distinguish between prejudice and discrimination.
- To provide examples of institutional prejudice and discrimination.
- To see how prejudice and discrimination combine to create a vicious cycle.
- To describe the histories and relative statuses of each of the racial and ethnic groups identified in the text.

PART III: KEY CONCEPTS

1. _____ refers to a socially constructed category composed of people who share biologically transmitted traits that members of a society consider important.
2. _____ is a shared cultural heritage.
3. A _____ is any category of people, distinguished by cultural or physical differences, that society sets apart and subordinates.
4. _____ refers to a rigid and irrational generalization about an entire category of people.
5. _____ is the belief that one racial category is innately superior or inferior to another.
6. A _____ is a person or category of people, typically with little power, who people unfairly blame for their own troubles.
7. _____ refers to any action that involves treating various categories of people unequally.
8. _____ _____ _____ _____ refers to bias inherent in the operation of society's institutions.
9. A state in which racial and ethnic groups are distinct but have social parity is known as _____.
10. _____ refers to the process by which minorities gradually adopt patterns of the dominant culture.
11. _____ refers to the biological reproduction by partners of different racial categories.
12. _____ is the physical and social separation of categories of people.
13. _____ refers to the systematic annihilation of one category of people by another.

PART IV: IMPORTANT RESEARCHERS

In the blank space below each of the following researchers, write two of three sentences to help you remember his or her respective contributions to sociology.

Thomas Sowell   Emory Bogardus

T. W. Adorno

PART V: STUDY QUESTIONS

True-False

1.   T   F   Although *racial categories* point to some biological elements, *race* is a socially constructed concept.
2.   T   F   According to the author of our text, for sociological purposes the concepts of *race* and *ethnicity* can be used interchangeably.
3.   T   F   Today's students express more social distance toward all minorities than students did decades ago.
4.   T   F   A racial or ethnic *minority* is a category of people, distinguished by physical or cultural traits, who are socially disadvantaged.
5.   T   F   The *scapegoat theory* links prejudice to frustration and suggests that prejudice is likely to be pronounced among people who themselves are disadvantaged.
6.   T   F   *Native Americans* were not granted citizenship in the United States until 1924.
7.   T   F   The *Dred Scott* Supreme Court decision declared that blacks were to have full rights and privileges as citizens of the United States.
8.   T   F   More than one-half of *Hispanics* in the United States are *Mexican Americans*.
9.   T   F   The highest rates of *immigration* to the United States occurred during the 1920s and 1930s.

Multiple Choice

1.   According to the text, which of the following may be the most integrated city in the United States?

      (a)   Houston, Texas
      (b)   Sacramento, California
      (c)   New York City
      (d)   Columbus, Ohio

2.   A socially constructed category composed of people who share biologically transmitted traits that members of a society deem socially significant is the definition for

(a)   race.
(b)   minority group.
(c)   ethnicity.
(d)   assimilation.

3.   Members of an *ethnic category* share

(a)   common ancestors, language, and religion.
(b)   only biological distinctions.
(c)   residential location.
(d)   social class ranking.

4.   Among people of *European descent,* the largest number of people in the U.S. trace their ancestry back to

(a)   Italy.
(b)   Ireland.
(c)   England.
(d)   Germany.

5.   *Minority groups* have two major characteristics,

(a)   race and ethnicity.
(b)   religion and ethnicity.
(c)   physical traits and political orientation.
(d)   sexual orientation and race.
(e)   distinctive identity and subordination.

6.   What is the term for a rigid and irrational generalization about an entire category of people?

(a)   racism
(b)   discrimination
(c)   stereotype
(d)   prejudice

7.   A *form of prejudice* referring to the belief that one racial category is innately superior or inferior to another is called

(a)   stereotyping.
(b)   discrimination.
(c)   racism.
(d)   scapegoating.

8.   One explanation of the origin of prejudice is found in the concept of the *authoritarian personality*. Such a personality exhibits

    (a)   an attitude of authority over others believed to be inferior.
    (b)   frustration over personal troubles directed toward someone less powerful.
    (c)   rigid conformity to conventional cultural norms and values.
    (d)   social distance from others deemed inferior.

9.   Treating various categories of people unequally refers to

    (a)   prejudice.
    (b)   stereotyping.
    (c)   miscegenation.
    (d)   discrimination.

10.   According to the work of W. I. Thomas, a *vicious circle* is formed by which variables?

    (a)   miscegenation and authoritarianism
    (b)   race and ethnicity
    (c)   pluralism and assimilation
    (d)   segregation and integration
    (e)   prejudice and discrimination

11.   A state in which racial and ethnic minorities are distinct but have social parity is termed

    (a)   segregation.
    (b)   pluralism.
    (c)   integration.
    (d)   assimilation.

12.   The process by which minorities gradually adopt patterns of the dominant culture is known as

    (a)   pluralism.
    (b)   amalgamation.
    (c)   assimilation.
    (d)   miscegenation.

13.   Which of the following statements is/are accurate concerning *white Anglo Saxon Protestants (WASPs)?*

    (a)   They represent about twenty percent of our nation's population.
    (b)   Historically, WASP immigrants were highly skilled and motivated to achieve by what we now call the Protestant work ethic.
    (c)   WASPs were never one single social group.
    (d)   The majority of people in the upper class in the United States are still WASPs.
    (e)   All of the above are accurate statements about WASPs.

14. In 1865, the _____ to the Constitution *outlawed slavery*.

    (a) Thirteenth Amendment
    (b) Civil Rights Act
    (c) Equal Rights Amendment
    (d) Twenty-sixth Amendment

15. *Jim Crow Laws*

    (a) protected freed slaves prior to the Civil War.
    (b) gave Native Americans residency rights west of the Mississippi.
    (c) integrated schools.
    (d) are examples of institutional discrimination.

Matching

1. ___ A socially constructed category composed of people who share biologically transmitted traits that members of a society consider important.
2. ___ A shared cultural heritage.
3. ___ A category of people, distinguished by physical or cultural traits, that is socially disadvantaged.
4. ___ A theory holding that prejudice springs from frustration among people who are themselves disadvantaged.
5. ___ An approach contending that while extreme prejudice may characterize some people, some prejudice is found in everyone.
6. ___ A state in which racial and ethnic minorities are distinct but have social parity.
7. ___ The process by which minorities gradually adopt patterns of the dominant culture.
8. ___ Non-WASPs whose ancestors lived in Ireland, Poland, Germany, Italy, or other European countries.

a.	assimilation	e.	cultural theory
b.	minority	f.	pluralism
c.	ethnicity	g.	race
d.	white ethnic Americans	h.	scapegoat theory

Fill-In

1. The term _____ refers to a socially constructed category composed of people who share biologically transmitted traits that members of society consider important.
2. While *race* is a _____ concept, *ethnicity* is a _____ concept.
3. Two major characteristics of *minorities* are that they have a _____ identity and are _____ by the social-stratification system.
4. _____ *theory* holds that prejudice springs from frustration.
5. Thomas Sowell has demonstrated that most of the documented racial difference in intelligence are not due to _____ but to people's _____.
6. _____ prejudice and discrimination refers to bias in attitudes or actions inherent in the operation of any of society's institutions.

7. In the _____ *case* of 1857, the U.S. Supreme Court addressed the question, "Are blacks citizens?" by writing "We think they are not...."
8. In 1865, the _____ _____ to the Constitution outlawed slavery.

Discussion

1. Differentiate between the concepts *prejudice* and *discrimination.*
2. What is *institutional prejudice and discrimination*? Provide two illustrations.
3. What are the four models representing the *patterns of interaction* between minority groups and the majority group? Define and discuss an illustration for each of these. In what three important ways did Japanese immigration and assimilation into U.S. society differ from the Chinese?
4   How do Native Americans, African Americans, Hispanic Americans, and Asian Americans compare to whites in terms of *educational achievement, family income,* and *poverty rates?*
5. What was the Court's ruling in *Brown vs. the Board of Education of Topeka case*?
6. What does the scientific evidence suggest about the relationship between *race* and *intelligence?*
7. How are the changing patterns in *immigration* likely to influence the future of the United States?
8. Do you think the United States is becoming more color blind or less color blind? Why?

PART VI: ANSWERS TO STUDY QUESTIONS

Key Concepts

1. Race (p. 280)
2. Ethnicity (p. 282)
3. minority (p. 283)
4. Prejudice (p. 284)
5. Racism (p. 287)
6. scapegoat (p. 287)
7. Discrimination (p. 289)
8. Institutional prejudice and discrimination (pp. 289-290)
9. pluralism (p. 290)
10. Assimilation (p. 291)
11. Miscegenation (p. 291)
12. Segregation (p. 291)
13. Genocide (p. 292)

True-False

1.	T	(p. 280)	6.	T	(p. 294)
2.	F	(p. 282)	7.	F	(p. 296)
3.	F	(p. 284)	8.	T	(p. 300)
4.	T	(p. 283)	9.	F	(p. 303)
5.	T	(p. 287)			

Multiple Choice

1.	b	(p. 280)	9.	d	(p. 289)
2.	a	(p. 280)	10.	e	(p. 290)
3.	a	(p. 282)	11.	b	(p. 290)
4.	d	(p. 283)	12.	c	(p. 291)
5.	e	(p. 283)	13.	e	(pp. 294-295)
6.	d	(p. 284)	14.	a	(p. 296)
7.	c	(p. 287)	15.	d	(p. 296)
8.	c	(p. 288)			

Matching

1.	g	(p. 280)	5.	e	(p. 288)
2.	c	(p. 282)	6.	f	(p. 290)
3.	b	(p. 283)	7.	a	(p. 291)
4.	h	(p. 287)	8.	d	(p. 303)

Fill-In
1. race (p. 280)
2. biological, cultural (p. 282)
3. distinctive, subordinated (p. 283)
4. Scapegoat (p. 287)
5. biology, environments (p. 288)
6. Institutional (pp. 289-290)
7. Dred Scott (pp. 295-296)
8. Thirteenth Amendment (p. 296)

PART VII: IN FOCUS--IMPORTANT ISSUES

- The Social Meaning of Race and Ethnicity

  Differentiate between the concepts of *race* and *ethnicity*.

  What are the basic characteristics of a *minority group*?

  How does discrimination differ from prejudice?

  Provide two illustrations of *institutional discrimination*.

113

- Majority and Minority: Patterns of Interaction

    Define and illustrate each of the following *patterns of interaction* between racial and ethnic groups.

        pluralism

        assimilation

        segregation

        genocide

- Race and Ethnicity in the United States

    Identify two important characteristics for the following racial and ethnic groups that differentially characterize them in our society's social stratification system.

        Native Americans

        White Anglo-Saxon Protestants

        African Americans

        Asian Americans

                Chinese Americans

                Japanese Americans

                recent Asian Immigrants

        Hispanic Americans

                Mexican Americans

                Puerto Ricans

                Cuban Americans

        White Ethnic Americans

114

- Race and Ethnicity: Looking Ahead

  What are the issues today that are different from the past concerning *immigration* to the United States?

Chapter	Economics
12	and Politics

PART I: CHAPTER OUTLINE

I.   The Economy: Historical Overview
      A.   The Agricultural Revolution
      B.   The Industrial Revolution
      C.   The Information Revolution and the Postindustrial Society
      D.   Sectors of the Economy
      E.   The Global Economy
II.   Economic Systems: Paths to Justice
      A.   Capitalism
      B.   Socialism
      C.   Welfare Capitalism and State Capitalism
      D.   Relative Advantages of Capitalism and Socialism
            1.   Economic Productivity
            2.   Economic Equality
            3.   Personal Freedom
      E.   Changes in Socialist Countries
III.   Work in the Postindustrial Economy
      A.   The Changing Workplace
      B.   Labor Unions
      C.   Professions
      D.   Self-Employment
      E.   Unemployment
      F.   Workplace Diversity: Race and Gender
      G.   New Information Technology and Work
IV.   Corporations
      A.   Economic Concentration
      B.   Corporate Linkages
      C.   Corporations: Are They Competitive?
      D.   Corporations and the Global Economy
      E.   Looking Ahead: The Economy of the Twenty-First Century
V.   Politics: Historical Overview
VI.   Global Political Systems
      A.   Monarchy
      B.   Democracy
      C.   Authoritarianism
      D.   Totalitarianism
      E.   A Global Political System?

PART II: LEARNING OBJECTIVES

- To identify the elements of the economy.
- To compare the economic systems of capitalism, state capitalism, socialism, and democratic socialism.
- To explain the difference between socialism and communism.
- To describe the general characteristics and trends of work in the U.S. postindustrial society.
- To compare the four principal kinds of political systems.
- To describe the nature of the American political system of government, and discuss the principal characteristics of the political spectrum of the U.S.
- To identify the factors that increase the likelihood of war.
- To recognize the historical pattern of militarism in the United States and around the world, and to consider factors that can be used to pursue peace.

PART III: KEY CONCEPTS

1.   A major sphere of social life, or societal system, designed to meet human needs is called a

     _____ _____.

2.	The _____ is the social institution that organizes a society's production, distribution, and consumption of goods and services.

3.	The _____ _____ refers to a productive system based on service work and high technology.

4.	The _____ _____ is the part of the economy that draws raw materials from the natural environment.

5.	The _____ _____ is the part of the economy that transforms raw materials into manufactured goods.

6.	The _____ _____ is the part of the economy involving services rather than goods.

7.	The _____ _____ refers to the expanding economic activity with little regard for national borders.

8.	_____ is an economic system in which natural resources and the means of producing goods and services are privately owned.

9.	_____ is an economic system in which natural resources and the means of producing goods and services are collectively owned.

10.	_____ _____ is an economic and political system that combines a mostly market-based economy with extensive social welfare programs.

11.	_____ _____ refers to an economic and political system in which companies are privately owned but cooperate closely with the government.

12.	A _____ is a prestigious white-collar occupation that requires extensive formal education.

13.	A _____ is an organization with a legal existence, including rights and liabilities, apart from those of its members.

14.	A _____ refers to the domination of a market by a single producer.

15.	A _____ refers to the domination of a market by a few producers.

16.	_____ refers to the social institution that distributes power, sets society's agenda, and makes decisions.

17.	_____ is the ability to achieve desired ends despite the resistance of others.

18.	A _____ is a formal organization that directs the political life of a society.

19.	_____ refers to power that people perceive as legitimate rather than coercive.

20.	The _____ ____ _____ is the transformation of charismatic authority into some combination of traditional and bureaucratic authority.

21.	A _____ is a type of political system in which a single family rules from generation to generation.

22.	A _____ is a type of political system that gives power to the people as a whole.

23.	_____ is a political system that denies popular participation in government.

24.	_____ refers to a highly centralized political system that extensively regulates people's lives.

25.	A _____ _____ refers to a range of government agencies and programs that provides benefits to the population.

26.	The _____ _____ refers to an analysis of politics that sees power as dispersed among many competing interest groups.

27.	The _____-_____ _____ refers to an analysis of politics that sees power as concentrated among the rich.

28.	The _____ _____-_____ _____ is an analysis that explains politics in terms of the operation of society's economic system.

29. A _____ _____ refers to the overthrow of one political system in order to establish another.

30. _____ refers to acts of violence or the threat of such violence by an individual or group as a political strategy.

31. _____ refers to organized, armed conflict between the peoples of various societies.

32. The close association of the federal government, the military, and the defense industries is referred to as the _____ - _____ _____.

PART IV: IMPORTANT RESEARCHERS

In the space below the following researcher's name, write two or three sentences to help you remember his or her contributions to sociology.

Karl Marx   Max Weber

Nelson Polsby   C. Wright Mills

Robert and Helen Lynd

PART V: STUDY QUESTIONS

<u>True-False</u>

1. T F The *economy* includes the production, distribution, and consumption of both goods and services.

2. T F *Agriculture*, as a subsistence strategy, first emerged some five thousand years ago.

3. T F The *secondary sector* of the economy is the part of the economy that generates raw material directly from the natural environment.

4. T F According to the text, the Information Revolution is changing the kind of work people do and where they do it. Part of the consequence of this process is that computers are *deskilling labor.*

5. T F *Authoritarianism* refers to a political system that denies popular participation in government.

6. T F *Voter apathy* is a problem, as evidenced by the fact that eligible citizens in the U.S. are less likely to vote today than they were a century ago.

7. T F One of the four insights offered concerning *terrorism* is that democracies are especially vulnerable to it because these governments afford extensive civil liberties to their people and have limited police networks.

8. T F In recent years, defense has been the largest single expenditure by the U.S. government, accounting for fifteen percent of federal spending.

Multiple Choice

1.	The *sector* of the economy that transforms raw materials into manufactured goods is termed the

    (a)	primary sector.
    (b)	competitive sector.
    (c)	secondary sector.
    (d)	basic sector.
    (e)	manifest sector.

2.	Your occupation is teaching. In what production *sector* of the economy do you work?

    (a)	primary
    (b)	secondary
    (c)	tertiary
    (d)	manifest

3.	Which of the following is/are accurate statements concerning *capitalism*?

    (a)	Justice, in a capitalist context, amounts to freedom of the marketplace where one can produce, invest, and buy according to individual self-interest.
    (b)	A purely capitalist economy is a free-market system with no government interference, sometimes called a laissez-faire economy.
    (c)	Consumers regulate a free-market economy.
    (d)	All are accurate statements concerning capitalism.

4.	Sweden and Italy represent what type of economic and political system?

    (a)	capitalism
    (b)	socialism
    (c)	communism
    (d)	welfare capitalism

5.	An economic and political system that combines a mostly market-based economy with extensive social welfare programs.

    (a)	socialism
    (b)	market socialism
    (c)	market communism
    (d)	an oligarchy
    (e)	welfare capitalism

6. During the 1970s, *socialist economies* had about _____ as much *income inequality* as was found in capitalist economies during the same time period.

   (a)   one-tenth
   (b)   twice
   (c)   three times
   (d)   one-half
   (e)   four times

7. A _____ is a prestigious, white-collar occupation that requires extensive formal education.

   (a)   profession
   (b)   career
   (c)   technical occupation
   (d)   primary sector work

8. What is the term for giant corporations composed of many smaller corporations?

   (a)   megacorporations
   (b)   monopolies
   (c)   multinational corporations
   (d)   conglomerates
   (e)   oligarchies

9. Power that people perceive as being *legitimate* rather than coercive is the definition for

   (a)   a monarchy.
   (b)   totalitarianism.
   (c)   government.
   (d)   politics.
   (e)   authority.

10. _____ refers to a highly centralized political system that extensively regulates people's lives.

   (a)   Authoritarianism
   (b)   Totalitarianism
   (c)   Absolute monarchy
   (d)   State capitalism

11. A _____ refers to a range of government agencies and programs that provides benefits to the population.

   (a)   socialist system
   (b)   democracy
   (c)   authoritarian government
   (d)   welfare state

12. Which idea below represents the *pluralist model* of power?

   (a)   Power is highly concentrated.
   (b)   Voting cannot create significant political changes.
   (c)   The U.S. power system is an oligarchy.
   (d)   Power is widely dispersed throughout society.

13. According to Paul Johnson, which of the following is/are distinguishing characteristics of *terrorism*?

   (a)   Terrorists try to paint violence as a legitimate political tactic.
   (b)   Terrorism is employed not just by groups, but by governments against their own people.
   (c)   Democratic societies reject terrorism in principle, but they are especially vulnerable to terrorists because they afford extensive civil liberties.
   (d)   Terrorism is always a matter of definition.
   (e)   all of the above

14. Quincy Wright has identified several circumstances as conditions that lead humans to go to war. Which of the following is *not* one of these?

   (a)   perceived threat
   (b)   political objectives
   (c)   social problems
   (d)   moral objectives
   (e)   wide-ranging alternatives

15. *Military spending* accounts for _____ percent of the federal budget of the United States.

   (a)   less than 5
   (b)   10
   (c)   18
   (d)   35

Matching

1. ____   The social institution that organizes a society's production, distribution, and consumption of goods and services.
2. ____   Economic activity spanning many nations of the world with little regard for national borders.
3. ____   An economic and political system in which companies are privately owned although they cooperate closely with the government.
4. ____   An organization with a legal existence, including rights and liabilities, apart from those of its members.
5. ____   A political system that denies popular participation in government.
6. ____   An analysis of politics that views power as concentrated among the rich.
7. ____   Random acts of violence or the threat of such violence by an individual or group as a political strategy.
8. ____   Organized, armed conflict among the people of various societies, directed by their government.

122

a.	state capitalism	e.	power-elite model
b.	economy	f.	war
c.	global economy	g.	authoritarianism
d.	corporation	h.	terrorism

Fill-In

1. *Industrialization* introduced five fundamental changes in the economies of Western societies, including: new forms of _____, the centralization of work in _____, manufacturing and _____ _____, _____, and _____ _____.

2. A _____ *economy* is a productive system based on service work and high technology.

3. A *socialist system* has three distinctive features, including: _____ ownership of property, pursuit of _____ goals, and _____ control of the economy.

4. People describe their occupations as *professions* to the extent that they demonstrate the following four characteristics: _____ knowledge, _____ practice, _____ over clients, and _____ orientation rather than to self-interest.

5. A _____ is a political system in which a single family rules from generation to generation.

6. _____ refers to a highly centralized political system that extensively regulates people's lives.

7. Analysts claim *revolutions* share a number of traits, including: rising _____, _____ government, _____ leadership by intellectuals, and establishing a new _____.

8. The most recent approaches to *peace* include: _____ __, high-technology _____, _____ and disarmament, and resolving underlying _____.

Discussion

1. Define the concept *postindustrial society*, and identify three key changes unleashed by the *Information Revolution*.

2. What are the three basic characteristics of *capitalism*? What are the three basic characteristics of *socialism*? What is *democratic socialism*? What are the relative advantages and disadvantages of each for members of a society?

3. What are the three main consequences of the development of a *global economy*?

4. Identify and discuss the major characteristics of a *postindustrial economy*.

5. Four types of *political systems* are reviewed in the text. Identify and describe each of these systems.

6. Discuss the *changing work place* using demographic data presented in the text. What are three changes that you think are positive? What are three changes you think are negative?

7. Differentiate between the *pluralist* and *power-elite* models concerning the distribution of power in the United States.

8. What are the five insights presented in the text concerning *terrorism*?

PART VI: ANSWERS TO STUDY QUESTIONS

Key Terms

1. social institution (p. 310)
2. economy (p. 310)
3. postindustrial economy (p. 312)
4. primary sector (p. (312)
5. secondary sector (p. 312)
6. tertiary sector (p. 312)
7. global economy (p. 313)
8. Capitalism (p. 314)
9. Socialism (p. 315)
10. Welfare capitalism (p. 316)
11. State capitalism (p. 316)
12. profession (p. 318)
13. corporation (p. 321)
14. monopoly (p. 322)
15. oligopoly (p. 322)
16. Politics (p. 324)
17. Power (pp. 324-25)
18. government (p. 325)
19. Authority (325)
20. routinization of charisma (p. 325)
21. monarchy (p. 326)
22. democracy (p. 326)
23. Authoritarianism (p. 326)
24. Totalitarianism (p. 328)
25. welfare state (p. 329)
26. pluralist model (p. 332)
27. power-elite model (p. 333)
28. Marxist political economy model (p. 333)
29. Political revolution (p. 334)
30. Terrorism (p. 335)
31. War (p. 335)
32. military-industrial complex (p. 337)

True-False

1.	T	(p. 310)	5.	T	(p. 326)
2.	T	(p. 311)	6.	T	(p. 331)
3.	F	(p. 312)	7.	T	(p. 335)
4.	T	(p. 320)	8.	F	(p. 337)

Multiple Choice

1.	c	(p. 312)	9.	e	(p. 325)
2.	c	(p. 312)	10.	b	(p. 328)
3.	d	(pp. 314-315)	11.	d	(p. 329)
4.	d	(p. 316)	12.	d	(p. 332)
5.	e	(p. 316)	13.	e	(p. 335)
6.	d	(p. 316)	14.	e	(p. 336)
7.	a	(p. 318)	15.	c	(p. 337)
8.	d	(p. 322)			

Matching

1.	b	(p. 310)	5.	g	(p. 326)
2.	c	(p. 313)	6.	e	(p. 333)
3.	a	(p. 316)	7.	h	(p. 335)
4.	d	(p. 321)	8.	f	(p. 335)

Fill-In

1. energy, factories, mass production, specialization, wage labor (p. 311)
2. postindustrial (p. 312)
3. collective, collective, government (p. 315)
4. theoretical, self-regulating, authority, community (pp. 318-319)
5. monarchy (p. 326)
6. Totalitarianism (p. 328)
7. expectations, unresponsive, radical, legitimacy (p. 334)
8. deterrence, defense, diplomacy, conflicts (p. 338)

PART VII: IN FOCUS—IMPORTANT ISSUES

- The Economy: Historical Overview

    Identify and describe the five fundamental ways in which *industrialization* changed the economy.

    What are the four major consequences of the *global economy*?

- Economic Systems: Paths to Justice

  What are the three distinctive features of *capitalism?*

      1.

      2.

      3.

  What are the three distinctive features of *socialism*?

      1.

      2.

      3.

- Work in the Postindustrial Economy

  Differentiate between the major qualities of *industrial society* and *postindustrial society*.

  What are the four ways in which *computers* are changing the character of work in the United States? Provide an illustration for each of these.

            change   illustration

      1.

      2.

      3.

      4.

- Corporations

  What is the evidence that there is *economic concentration* in the United States?

- Looking Ahead: The Economy of the Twenty-First Century

  What are three major patterns that are expected to continue to occur in terms of our economy?

    1.

    2.

    3.

- Global Political Systems

  Define and illustrate each of the categories of *political systems.*

- Politics in the United States

  Describe the *political spectrum* in the United States. What strikes you most about the data presented in the text?

- Theoretical Analysis of Politics

  Differentiate among the following competing models of power in the United States. What evidence is used to support each model?

    pluralist model

    power-elite model

    Marxist model

- Power Beyond the Rules

     What are the four traits commonly shared by *revolutions?*

     What are the four distinguishing characteristics of *terrorism?*

- War and Peace

     Identify and illustrate five factors that promote *war.*

     What are the four recent approaches to *peace* identified in the text? What are your thoughts on each in terms of promoting peace?

- Looking Ahead: Politics in the Twenty-First Century

     What are the four *global trends* being identified by the author?

Chapter

13 | Family and Religion

PART I: CHAPTER OUTLINE

I.   The Family: Basic Concepts
II.   The Family: Global Variations
    A.   Marriage Patterns
    B.   Residential Patterns
    C.   Patterns of Descent
    D.   Patterns of Authority
III. Theoretical Analysis of the Family
    A.   Functions of the Family: Structural-Functional Analysis
    B.   Inequality and the Family: Social-Conflict Analysis
    C.   Constructing Family Life: Micro-Level Analysis
        1.   The Symbolic-Interaction Approach
        2.   The Social-Exchange Approach
IV.   Stages of Family Life
    A.   Courtship and Romantic Love
    B.   Settling In: Ideal and Real Marriage
    C.   Child Rearing
    D.   The Family in Later Life
V.   U.S. Families: Class, Race, and Gender
    A.   Social Class
    B.   Ethnicity and Race
        1.   American Indian Families
        2.   Latino Families
        3.   African-American Families
        4.   Ethnically and Racially Mixed Marriages
    C.   Gender
VI.   Transitions and Problems in Family Life
    A.   Divorce
        1.   Causes of Divorce
        2.   Who Divorces?
    B.   Remarriage
    C.   Family Violence
        1.   Violence Against Women
        2.   Violence Against Children
VII. Alternative Family Forms
    A.   One-Parent Families
    B.   Cohabitation

PART II: LEARNING OBJECTIVES

- To define and illustrate basic concepts relating to the social institutions of kinship, family, and marriage.
- To gain a cross-cultural perspective of the social institutions of kinship, family, and marriage.
- To analyze the social institutions of kinship, family, and marriage using the structural-functional, social-conflict, and symbolic-interaction perspectives.
- To describe the traditional life course of the U.S. family.
- To recognize the impact of social class, race, ethnicity, and gender socialization on the family.
- To define basic concepts relating to the sociological analysis of religion.
- To describe how industrialization and science affect religious beliefs and practices.
- To discuss the basic demographic patterns concerning religious affiliation, religiosity, secularization, and religious revival in the U.S. today.

PART III: KEY CONCEPTS

1. The _____ is a social institution found in all societies that unites people in cooperative groups to oversee the bearing and raising of children.
2. _____ refers to a social bond based on blood, marriage, or adoption.
3. A _____ _____ is a social group of two or more people, related by blood, marriage, or adoption, who usually live together.
4. _____ refers to a legally sanctioned relationship, usually involving economic cooperation as well as sexual activity and childbearing that people expect to be enduring.
5. An _____ _____ is a family unit that includes parents and children as well as other kin.
6. A _____ _____ is a family unit composed of one or two parents and their children.
7. _____ refers to marriage between people of the same social category.
8. _____ refers to marriage between people of different social categories.
9. Marriage that unites two partners is known as _____.
10. Marriage that unites three or more people refers to _____.
11. _____ refers to the system by which members of a society trace kinship over generations.
12. The _____ _____ is a norm forbidding sexual relations or marriage between certain relatives.
13. Marriage between people with the same social characteristics is known as _____.
14. The sharing of a household by an unmarried couple is known as _____.
15. The _____ refers to that which people define as an ordinary element of everyday life.
16. The _____ refers to that which people set apart as extraordinary, inspiring a sense of awe and reverence.
17. _____ is a social institution involving beliefs and practices based on a conception of the sacred.
18. _____ refers to belief anchored in conviction rather than scientific evidence.
19. A _____ is an object in the natural world collectively defined as sacred.
20. _____ _____ is a fusion of Christian principles with political activism, often Marxist in character.
21. A _____ is a type of religious organization well integrated into the larger society.
22. A _____ _____ is a church formally allied with the state.
23. A _____ is a church, independent of the state, that accepts religious pluralism.
24. A _____ is a type of religious organization that stands apart from the larger society.
25. _____ refers to extraordinary personal qualities that can turn an audience into followers.
26. A _____ is a religious organization that is largely outside a society's cultural traditions.
27. _____ refers to the belief that elements of the natural world are conscious life forms that affect humans.
28. The importance of religion in a person's life is known as _____.
29. _____ refers to the historical decline in the importance of the supernatural and the sacred.
30. A _____ _____ is a quasi-religious loyalty, binding individuals in a basically secular society.
31. _____ refers to a conservative religious doctrine that opposes intellectualism and worldly accommodation in favor of restoring traditional, otherworldly religion.

PART IV: IMPORTANT RESEARCHERS

In the space provided below each of the following researchers, write two or three sentences to help you remember his or her respective contributions to sociology.

Lillian Rubin   Jessie Bernard

Emile Durkheim   Karl Marx

Max Weber

PART V: STUDY QUESTIONS

True-False

1.	T	F	Norms of *endogamy* relate to marriage between people of the same social category.
2.	T	F	While the *divorce rate* in the U.S. is high; relative to other industrialized societies it is fairly low.
3.	T	F	*Blended families* are composed of children and some combination of biological parents and stepparents.
4.	T	F	Less than one-third of those couples who *cohabit* eventually marry.
5.	T	F	According to Emile Durkheim, the *profane* refers to that which is an ordinary element of everyday life.
6.	T	F	A major criticism of Emile Durkheim's analysis of religion is that he focuses too much attention on the *dysfunctions* of religious belief and practice.
7.	T	F	Whereas a *cult* is a type of religious organization that stands apart from the larger society, a *sect* represents something almost entirely new and stands outside a society's cultural tradition.
8.	T	F	Science and new technologies are reducing the relevance of religion in modern society as many moral dilemmas and spiritual issues are resolved or are diminishing in significance.

Multiple Choice

1.   Which of the following concepts refers to a social bond, based on blood, marriage, or adoption?

    (a)   descent group
    (b)   nuclear family
    (c)   family
    (d)   kinship

132

2.   What is the family unit including parents and children, as well as other kin?

   (a)   a family
   (b)   a kinship group
   (c)   a nuclear family
   (d)   an extended family

3.   What is the system by which members of a society trace kinship over generations?

   (a)   descent
   (b)   family
   (c)   marriage
   (d)   extended family

4.   Which theory and theorist traced the origin of the family to the need for men to pass property on to their sons?

   (a)   symbolic-interaction--George Herbert Mead
   (b)   structural-functionalism--Talcott Parsons
   (c)   structural-functionalism--Emile Durkheim
   (d)   social-conflict--Friedrich Engels

5.   Lillian Rubin focused her research on the relationship between _____ and marriage.

   (a)   social class
   (b)   race
   (c)   presence of children
   (d)   age at marriage

6.   The high U.S. *divorce rate* has many causes. Which of the following is *not* identified in the text as being one of them?

   (a)   Individualism is on the rise.
   (b)   Women are more dependent on men.
   (c)   Many marriages today are stressful.
   (d)   Romantic love often subsides.
   (e)   Divorce is easier to get and more socially acceptable.

7.   Currently in the U.S., what percentage of children are living in *single-parent families*?

   (a)   16
   (b)   45
   (c)   9
   (d)   27

8.   Cohabiting tends to appeal more to

(a)   traditionally-minded people.
(b)   those who reject marriage.
(c)   those who favor gender equity.
(d)   Roman Catholics.
(e)   those who intend to remain single.

9.   Which country, in 1989, became the first nation to legalize *same-sex marriages*?

(a)   Denmark
(b)   France
(c)   the United States
(d)   Japan

10.   Emile Durkheim referred to the ordinary elements of everyday life as

(a)   religion.
(b)   faith.
(c)   ritual.
(d)   the profane.

11.   Which of the following is an appropriate criticism of a *symbolic-interactionist's* approach to the study of religion?

(a)   It ignores religion's link to inequality.
(b)   It fails to consider the importance of rituals.
(c)   It treats reality as objective.
(d)   It ignores the social construction of religion.

12.   *Liberation theology* advocates a blending of religion with

(a)   the family.
(b)   the economy.
(c)   education.
(d)   political activism.

13.   A religious organization that is largely outside society's cultural traditions is called a

(a)   totem.
(b)   cult.
(c)   ecclesia.
(d)   sect.

14. What is *secularization*?

   (a)   the ecumenical movement
   (b)   the historical decline in the importance of the supernatural and the sacred
   (c)   the increase in religiosity in postindustrial society
   (d)   fundamentalism

15. Which of the following is *not* identified in the text as a distinctive ingredient of *religious fundamentalism*?

   (a)   Fundamentalists interpret sacred texts literally.
   (b)   Fundamentalists promote religious pluralism.
   (c)   Fundamentalists pursue the personal experience of God's presence.
   (d)   Fundamentalism opposes "secular humanism."
   (e)   Many fundamentalists endorse conservative political goals.

Matching

1. ____   A family unit including parents and children, as well as other kin.
2. ____   The social institution involving beliefs and practices based on a conception of the sacred.
3. ____   Belief anchored in conviction rather than scientific evidence.
4. ____   Marriage between people of the same social category.
5. ____   The importance of religion in a person's life.
6. ____   The historical decline in the importance of the supernatural and the sacred.
7. ____   A system tracing kinship through both men and women.
8. ____   The feeling of affection and sexual passion toward another person as the basis of marriage.

   a.   endogamy   e.   secularization
   b.   religion   f.   bilateral descent
   c.   religiosity   g.   faith
   d.   romantic love   h.   extended family

Fill-In

1. _____ refers to the system by which members of a society trace kinship over generations.
2. *Social-conflict* theorists argue that families perpetuate social inequality in several ways, including: property and _____, _____, and _____.
3. The high U.S. *divorce rate* has many causes, including: _____ is on the rise, _____ _____ often subsides, women are now less _____ on men, many of today's marriages are _____, divorce is more socially _____, and legally, divorce is _____ to obtain.
4. _____ is the sharing of a household by an unmarried couple.
5. Emile Durkheim labeled the ordinary elements of everyday life the _____.
6. A _____ is a type of religious organization well integrated into the larger society.
7. _____ refers to extraordinary personal qualities that can turn audiences into followers.

8.   *Religious fundamentalism* is distinctive in five ways, including: interpreting sacred texts _____, rejecting religious _____, pursuing the personal experience of God's _____, opposition to secular _____, and endorsement of _____ political goals.

Discussion

1.   Why has the *divorce rate* increased in recent decades in the United States? What are the basic demographic patterns involving divorce in our society today?
2.   What are the four *stages* of the family life cycle outlined in the text? Describe the major events occurring during each of these stages.
3.   What are the arguments being made about the family by *social-conflict* theorists?
4.   What are the five conclusions being made about marriage and family life in the twenty-first century?
5.   According to *structural-functional* analysis, what are three major functions of religion? Provide an example for each from U.S. society.
6.   Discuss the relationship between *religion* and *social stratification* in the United States today.
7.   Differentiate between *civil religion* and *religious fundamentalism*.
8.   Discuss the issue concerning the extent of *religiosity* in the United States today.

PART V: ANSWERS TO STUDY QUESTIONS

Key Concepts

1.   family (p. 346)
2.   Kinship (p. 346)
3.   family unit (p. 346)
4.   Marriage (p. 347)
5.   extended family (p. 347)
6.   nuclear family (p. 347)
7.   Endogamy (p. 347)
8.   Exogamy (p. 347)
9.   monogamy (p. 347)
10. polygamy (p. 347)
11. Descent (p. 349)
12. incest taboo (p. 349)
13. homogamy (p. 352)
14. cohabitation (p. 359)
15. profane (p. 363)
16. sacred (p. 363)
17. Religion (p. 363)
18. Faith (p. 364)
19. totem (p. 364)
20. Liberation theology (p. 367)
21. church (p. 367)
22. state church (p. 368)
23. denomination (p. 368)
24. sect (p. 368)

25. Charisma (p. 368)
26. cult (p. 369)
27. Animism (p. 369)
28. religiosity (p. 370)
29. Secularization (p. 372)
30. civil religion (p. 372)
31. Fundamentalism (p. 374)

True-False

1.	T	(p. 347)	5.	T	(p. 363)
2.	F	(p. 357)	6.	F	(p. 365)
3.	T	(p. 358)	7.	F	(pp. 368-369)
4.	F	(p. 360)	8.	F	(pp. 375-376)

Multiple Choice

1.	d	(p. 346)	9.	a	(p. 360)
2.	d	(p. 347)	10.	d	(p. 363)
3.	a	(p. 349)	11.	a	(p. 365)
4.	d	(p. 350)	12.	d	(p. 367)
5.	a	(p. 354)	13.	b	(p. 369
6.	b	(pp. 357-358)	14.	b	(p. 372
7.	d	(p. 359)	15.	b	(pp. 374-375
8.	c	(p. 353)			

Matching

1.	h	(p. 347)	5.	c	(p. 370)
2.	b	(p. 363)	6.	e	(p. 372)
3.	g	(p. 364)	7.	f	(p. 349)
4.	a	(p. 347)	8.	d	(p. 352)

Fill-In

1. Descent (p. 349)
2. inheritance, patriarchy, race and ethnicity (p. 350)
3. individualism, romantic love, dependent, stressful, acceptable, easier (pp. 357-358)
4. Cohabitation (p. 359)
5. profane (p. 363)
6. church (p. 367)
7. Charisma (p. 368)
8. literally, pluralism, presence, humanism, conservative (pp. 374-375)

PART VII: IN FOCUS--IMPORTANT ISSUES

- The Family: Basic Concepts

    What does the author mean by saying that there is a trend toward a more *inclusive* definition of the family?

- The Family: Global Variations

    Identify and define or illustrate the different *patterns* found around the world for each of the following:

    marriage

    residence

    descent

    authority

- Theoretical Analysis of the Family

    According to structural-functionalists, what are the *functions* performed by families? Provide one piece of evidence for each function.

    In what ways do *conflict theorists* believe the family perpetuates inequality? Illustrate or define each of these.

    Micro-level approaches explore how individuals shape and experience family life. Differentiate between the following two micro-level perspectives.

    symbolic-interaction analysis

    social-exchange analysis

- Stages of Family Life

    Briefly describe the content for each of the following stages in family life:

        courtship and romantic love

        settling in

        child rearing

        the family in later life

- U.S. Families: Class, Race, and Gender

    Summarize the findings concerning Lillian Rubin's research on the relationship between *social class* and the family.

- Transitions and Problems in Family Life

    Identify the major causes of *divorce* as listed in the text.

    How common is *remarriage*?

- Alternative Family Forms

    Identify two important demographic facts concerning *single-parent families* in our society today.

    How common is *cohabitation* in our society today?

    What are two important points being made about *gay and lesbian couples*?

    How common is *singlehood* in our society today?

- New Reproductive Technology and the Family

    What is *in vitro fertilization*?

- Looking Ahead: The Family in the Twenty-First Century

    What are the five likely trends for the family of the twenty-first century as identified by the author?

- Religion: Basic Concepts

    Provide an illustration for Emile Durkheim's distinction between the *profane* and the *sacred*.

- Theoretical Analysis of Religion

    According to *structural-functionalist* Emile Durkheim, what are the three basic *functions of religion*?

    What points are being made by *symbolic-interactionist* Peter Berger concerning religion?

    How did *conflict theorist* Karl Marx understand religion?

- Religion and Social Change

    What is Max Weber's point concerning the relationship between *Protestantism* and *capitalism*?

- Types of Religious Organization

    Differentiate among each of the following:

        church

        sect

        cult

- Religion in History

    How is religion different in *preindustrial societies* as compared with industrial societies? What are the similarities?

- Religion in the United States

    How religious are we here in the United States? What is the evidence?

- Religion in a Changing Society

    Briefly discuss the place of each of the following patterns in the United States today.

        secularism

        civil religion

        religious revival

        religious fundamentalism

- Looking Ahead: Religion in the Twenty-First Century

    What conclusions are being made by the author concerning the place of religion in contemporary American society?

14 Education and Medicine

PART I: CHAPTER OUTLINE

I.   Education: A Global Survey
    A.   Schooling and Economic Development
    B.   Schooling in India
    C.   Schooling in Japan
    D.   Schooling in the United States

II.   The Functions of Schooling

III.   Schooling and Social Inequality
    A.   Public and Private Education
    B.   Access to Higher Education
    C.   Greater Opportunity: Expanding Higher Education
        1.   Community Colleges
    D.   Privilege and Personal Merit

IV.   Problems in the Schools
    A.   Discipline and Violence
    B.   Student Passivity
        1.   The Silent College Classroom
    C.   Dropping Out
    D.   Academic Standards
    E.   Grade Inflation

V.   Recent Issues in U.S. Education
    A.   School Choice
    B.   Home Schooling
    C.   Schooling People with Disabilities
    D.   Adult Education
    E.   The Teacher Shortage
    F.   Looking Ahead: Schooling in the Twenty-First Century

VI.   Medicine and Health
    A.   Health and Society

VII.   Health: A Global Survey
    A.   Health in Low-Income Countries
    B.   Health in High-Income Countries

VIII.   Health in the United States
    A.   Who Is Healthy? Age, Gender, Class, and Race
        1.   Social Epidemiology
        2.   Age and Gender
        3.   Social Class and Race

PART II: LEARNING OBJECTIVES

- To understand the relationship between schooling and economic development.
- To describe the different role of education in low-income and high-income countries.
- To consider how education supports social inequality.

- To discuss the major issues and problems facing contemporary education in the United States today.
- To recognize how race, social class, and age affect the health of individuals in our society.
- To describe the role of health care in low-income and in high-income nations.
- To discuss cigarette smoking, eating disorders, and sexually transmitted diseases as serious health problems in our society.
- To be familiar with the medical establishment on a global level.
- To begin to understand the viewpoints being provided by the three major sociological perspectives.

PART III: KEY CONCEPTS

1. _____ refers to the social institution through which society provides its members with important knowledge, including basic facts, job skills, and cultural norms and values.

2. Formal instruction under the direction of specially trained teachers is known as _____.

3. Assigning students to different types of educational programs is called _____.

4. _____ _____ refers to a lack of reading and writing skills needed for everyday living.

5. The social institution that focuses on combating disease and improving health is known as _____.

6. _____ is a state of complete physical, mental, and social well-being.

7. _____ _____ is the study of how health and disease are distributed throughout a society's population.

8. _____ refers to assisting in the death of a person suffering from an incurable disease.

9. _____ _____ is an approach to health care that emphasizes prevention of illness and takes into account a person's entire physical and social environment.

10. _____ _____ is a medical care system in which the government owns and operates most medical facilities and employs most physicians.

11. A _____-_____ _____ is a medical care system in which patients pay directly for the services of physicians and hospitals.

12. A _____ _____ _____ is an organization that provides comprehensive medical care to subscribers for a fixed fee.

13. The _____ _____ refers to patterns of behavior defined as appropriate for those who are ill.

PART IV: IMPORTANT RESEARCHERS

In the space provided below each of the following researchers, write two or three sentences to help you remember his or her respective contributions to the field of sociology.

David Karp and William Yoels   Randall Collins

James Coleman   Talcott Parsons

PART V: STUDY QUESTIONS

True-False

1.　T　　F　　Today, schooling in *low-income nations* reflects the diversity of their cultures.
2.　T　　F　　The United States graduates a *smaller percentage* of its students from high school than does Japan; however, Japan, because of competitive examinations, sends a smaller percentage of students on to college.
3.　T　　F　　The *Coleman Report* determined that the amount of educational funding was the most important factor in determining education achievement.
4.　T　　F　　The work *A Nation at Risk* focuses on the increasing violence in American schools.
5.　T　　F　　The World Health Organization defines *health* as simply the absence of disease.
6.　T　　F　　The top five *causes of death* in the U.S. have changed very little since 1900.
7.　T　　F　　Approximately seventy percent of all global *HIV cases* are recorded in sub-Saharan Africa.
8.　T　　F　　*Holistic medicine* stresses that physicians have to take the primary responsibility for health care in society.

Multiple Choice

1.　The social institution guiding a society's transmission of knowledge--including basic facts, job skills, and also cultural norms and values--to its members is the definition for

　　(a)　schooling.
　　(b)　teaching.
　　(c)　education.
　　(d)　curriculum.

2.　Which of the following is *inaccurate* concerning India?

　　(a)　People earn about five percent of the income standard in the United States, and poor families often depend on the earnings of children.
　　(b)　Less than one-half of Indian children enter secondary school.
　　(c)　About one-half of the Indian population is illiterate.
　　(d)　More girls than boys in India reach secondary school.

3.　Which of the following nations has the highest percentage of adults with a *college degree*?

　　(a)　United States
　　(b)　Netherlands
　　(c)　Canada
　　(d)　Denmark
　　(e)　Sweden

145

4. *Social-conflict analysis* uses the term _____ to refer to the assignment of students to different types of educational programs.

    (a)   hierarchical education
    (b)   residual education
    (c)   ability placement
    (d)   competitive placement
    (e)   tracking

5. The *Coleman Report* concluded that

    (a)   social inequality is not a problem in public education within our society.
    (b)   the simple answer to quality education is more funding for schools.
    (c)   minority schools are actually better than schools that are predominately white schools in terms of their student achievement.
    (d)   education is the great equalizer, and stressing the importance of differences between families is not particularly important for educational achievement.
    (e)   schools alone cannot overcome social inequality.

6. There are _____ colleges and universities in the United States.

    (a)   2,000
    (b)   3,000
    (c)   4,000
    (d)   5,000
    (e)   6,000

7. *Functional illiteracy* refers to

    (a)   an inability to read and write at all.
    (b)   an inability to read at the appropriate level of schooling based on one's age.
    (c)   an inability to effectively communicate abstract ideas.
    (d)   reading and writing skills insufficient for everyday living.

8. The *school choice* model focuses on the idea of

    (a)   competition.
    (b)   consensus.
    (c)   science.
    (d)   integration.

9. The *health* of any population is shaped by

    (a)   the society's cultural standards.
    (b)   the society's technology.
    (c)   the society's social inequality.
    (d)   all of the above

10. _____ is the study of how health and disease are distributed throughout a society's population.

   (a) Demography
   (b) Social epidemiology
   (c) Epistomolgy
   (d) Medicalization

11. Which of the following were the *leading causes of death* in the U.S. in 1900?

   (a) accidents and heart disease
   (b) cancer and diphtheria
   (c) influenza and pneumonia
   (d) lung disease and kidney disease
   (e) homicide and diabetes

12. According to medical experts, about how many people die prematurely in the U.S. each year as a direct result of *smoking*?

   (a) 100,000
   (b) 50,000
   (c) 200,000
   (d) 1 million
   (e) 440,000

13. Assisting in the death of a person suffering from an incurable disease is known as

   (a) annihilation.
   (b) amniocentesis.
   (c) genocide.
   (d) euthanasia.

14. Which country does *not* offer a comprehensive health program to the entire population?

   (a) Sweden
   (b) Great Britain
   (c) The United States
   (d) Canada

15. Which of the following *theoretical approaches* in sociology utilizes concepts like *sick role* and *physician's role* to help explain health behavior?

   (a) social-conflict
   (b) social-exchange
   (c) symbolic-interaction
   (d) cultural materialism
   (e) structural-functional

147

Matching

1. ____ The percentage of high school graduates in the U.S. who go on to college.
2. ____ The percentage of available nursing jobs that were unfilled in 2002.
3. ____ The number one cause of death in the U.S. today.
4. ____ Schooling in the U.S. reflects the value of _____.
5. ____ A medical care system in which the government owns most facilities and employs most physicians.
6. ____ The social institution that focuses on combating disease and improving health.
7. ____ An approach to health care that emphasizes prevention of illness and takes account of the person's entire physical and social environment.
8. ____ Confirmed that predominately minority schools suffer problems, but cautioned that money alone will not magically improve academic quality.

a.	socialized medicine	e.	medicine
b.	62	f.	heart disease
c.	practical learning	g.	James Coleman
d.	11	h.	holistic medicine

Fill-In

1. The social institution through which society provides its members with important knowledge, including basic facts, job skills, and cultural values and norms, is termed _____.
2. Although only _____ percent of U.S. school children are *bused to schools outside their neighborhoods for racial balance purposes*, this policy has generated heated controversy.
3. The most crucial factor affecting access to U.S. higher education is _____.
4. Four alternative approaches to increasing *school choice* include giving _____ to families with school-aged children and allowing them to spend that money on any school they want, _____ schools, schooling for _____, and _____ schools.
5. Society shapes the *health* of people in four major ways. These include: Cultural patterns define _____; cultural _____ of health change over time; a society's _____ affects people's health; and, social _____ affects people's health.
6. *Social* _____ is the study of how health and disease are distributed throughout a society's population.
7. Specific behaviors put people at high risk for *HIV* infection. These include _____ sex, sharing _____, and using any _____.
8. One strength of the _____ *approach* lies in revealing that what people view as healthful or harmful depends on numerous factors, many of which are not, strictly speaking, medical.

Discussion

1. What are the functions of schooling?
2. What recommendations were made in the report *A Nation at Risk*?
3. What are the major *problems* in U.S. education? Identify the specific factors involved in each problem identified. What is one recommendation you have for solving each of the problems?

4. What are the alternative approaches identified as ways of increasing *school choice*? What are your opinions on each of these?
5. How have the *causes of death* changed in the U.S. over the last century?
6. What is meant by the *sick role*?
7. What are *social-conflict* analysts' arguments about the health care system in the United States?
8. What do *symbolic-interactionists* mean by *socially constructing illness* and *socially constructing treatment*?

PART VII: ANSWERS TO STUDY QUESTIONS

Key Concepts

1. Education (p. 376)
2. schooling (p. 376)
3. tracking (p. 380)
4. Functional illiteracy (p. 387)
5. medicine (p. 390)
6. Health (p. 390)
7. Social epidemiology (p. 392)
8. Euthanasia (mercy killing) (p. 398)
9. Holistic medicine (pp. 399-400)
10. Socialized medicine (p. 400)
11. direct-fee system (p. 401)
12. health maintenance organization (HMO) (p. 401)
13. sick role (p. 403)

True-False

1.	T	(p. 376)	5.	F	(p. 390)
2.	T	(p. 378)	6.	F	(p. 391)
3.	F	(p. 381)	7.	T	(p. 396)
4.	F	(p. 387)	8.	F	(p. 400)

Multiple Choice

1.	c	(p. 376)	9.	d	(p. 390)
2.	d	(pp. 376-378)	10.	b	(p. 392)
3.	a	(p. 378)	11.	c	(p. 391)
4.	e	(p. 380)	12.	e	(p. 394)
5.	e	(p. 381)	13.	d	(p. 398)
6.	c	(p. 382)	14.	c	(p. 401)
7.	d	(p. 387)	15.	e	(p. 403)
8.	a	(p. 388)			

Matching

1. b   (p. 378)   5. a   (p. 400)
2. d   (p. 402)   6. e   (p. 390)
3. f   (p. 391)   7. h   (pp. 399-400)
4. c   (p. 379)   8. g   (p. 381)

Fill-In

1. education (p. 376)
2. 5 (p. 381)
3. money (p. 381)
4. vouchers, magnet, profit, charter (p. 388)
5. health, standards, technology, inequality (p. 390)
6. epidemiology (p. 392)
7. anal, needles, drugs (p. 396)
8. symbolic-interaction (p. 403)

PART VII: IN FOCUS--IMPORTANT ISSUES

- Education: A Global Survey

    Briefly characterize *schooling* in each of the following countries:

        India

        Japan

        United States

- The Functions of Schooling

    Illustrate each of the following *functions of schooling:*

        socialization

        cultural innovation

        social integration

        social placement

        latent functions

150

- Schooling and Social Inequality

    In what ways do social-conflict theorists believe each of the following lead to social inequality in schooling?

        social control

        standardized testing

        school tracking

    Briefly summarize the findings of the *Coleman Report.* How should these finding be interpreted for the purposes of educational policy?

- Problems in the Schools

    What is the evidence that schools have problems in the following areas?

        discipline and violence

        student passivity

        dropping out

        academic standards

        grade inflation

    What were the findings and conclusions of the study *A Nation at Risk*? What do you think needs to be done in terms of educational reform based on these findings?

- Recent Issues in U.S. Education

    Describe each of the following alternatives for *school choice:*

        vouchers

        magnet schools

schooling for profit

charter schools

home schooling

What are the arguments for and against these *school choice* alternatives?

- Looking Ahead: Schooling in the Twenty-First Century

  What are three important issues confronting schools over the next generation?

- What is Health?

  What are the four major ways in which society shapes people's *health*?

- Health: A Global Survey

  Generally describe the health of people living in *low-income countries*.

  What was the impact of *industrialization* on health in the U.S. and Europe?

- Health in the United States

  Briefly discuss the health patterns found in the United States using the following variables:

  age and gender

  social class and race

How significant a health problem is each of the following? Provide demographic evidence of illness and disease for each as discussed in the text.

cigarette smoking

eating disorders

sexually transmitted diseases

According to legal and medical experts, how is *death* defined?

Do people have the *right to die*?

What are the laws in the United States concerning *euthanasia*? What is your opinion on this issue?

- The Medical Establishment

Describe the impact of the rise of *scientific medicine* on health care in the United States.

What are the components of *holistic medicine*?

Briefly summarize how medical care is paid for in the following *socialist societies:*

The People's Republic of China

The Russian Federation

Briefly summarize how medical care is paid for in the following *capitalist societies:*

Sweden

Great Britain

Canada

Japan

How expensive is medical care in the United States? How do we pay for this medical care?

- Theoretical Analysis of Health and Medicine

  According to structural-functionalist analysis, what are the components of the *sick role*?

  What is the *physician's role*?

  What do symbolic-interactionists mean by the *social construction of illness*?

  According to social-conflict analysts, what are the three ways in which health care is related to *social inequality*? Describe and illustrate each of these.

- Looking Ahead: Health and Medicine in the Twenty-First Century

  Identify and describe the four *trends* identified by the author concerning health and health care in the U.S. over the next several decades.

Chapter 15 Population, Urbanization, and Environment

PART I: CHAPTER OUTLINE

I.   Demography: The Study of Population
    A.   Fertility
    B.   Mortality
    C.   Migration
    D.   Population Growth
    E.   Population Composition

II.   History and Theory of Population Growth
    A.   Malthusian Theory
    B.   Demographic Transition Theory
    C.   Global Population Today: A Brief Survey
         1.   The Low-Growth North
         2.   The High-Growth South

III.   Urbanization: The Growth of Cities
    A.   The Evolution of Cities
         1.   The First Cities
         2.   Preindustrial European Cities
         3.   Industrial European Cities
    B.   The Growth of U.S. Cities
         1.   Colonial Settlement: 1565-1800
         2.   Urban Expansion: 1800-1860
         3.   The Metropolitan Era: 1860-1950
         4.   Urban Decentralization: 1950-Present
    C.   Suburbs and Urban Decline
    D.   Postindustrial Sunbelt Cities
    E.   Megalopolis: Regional Cities
    F.   Edge Cities
    G.   The Rural Rebound

IV.   Urbanization as a Way of Life
    A.   Ferdinand Tönnies: Gemeinschaft and Gesellschaft
    B.   Emile Durkheim: Mechanical and Organic Solidarity
    C.   Georg Simmel: The Blasé Urbanite
    D.   The Chicago School: Robert Park and Louis Wirth
    E.   Urban Ecology
    F.   Urban Political Economy

PART II: LEARNING OBJECTIVES

- To learn the basic concepts used by demographers to study populations.
- To compare Malthusian theory and demographic transition theory.
- To gain an understanding of the worldwide urbanization process, and to be able to put it into historical perspective.
- To describe demographic changes in the U.S. throughout its history.
- To consider urbanism as a way of life as viewed by several historical figures in sociology.
- To consider the idea of urban ecology.
- To develop an understanding of how sociology can help us confront environmental issues.
- To be able to discuss the dimensions of the "logic of growth" and the "limits to growth" as issues and realities confronting our world.
- To identify and discuss major environmental issues confronting our world today.

PART III: KEY CONCEPTS

1. _____ is the study of human population.
2. _____ refers to the incidence of childbearing in a country's population.
3. The _____ _____ _____ refers to the number of live births in a given year for every thousand people in the population.
4. _____ refers to the incidence of death in a country's population.

156

5. The _____ _____ _____ refers to the number of deaths in a given year for every thousand people in a population.

6. The _____ _____ _____ refers to the number of deaths among infants under one year of age for each thousand live births in a given year.

7. _____ _____ refers to the average life span of a country's population.

8. The movement of people into and out of a specified territory is known as _____.

9. The _____ _____ refers to the number of males for every hundred females in a nation's population.

10. An _____ _____ is a graphic representation of the age and sex of a population.

11. _____ _____ _____ is the thesis that population patterns reflect a society's level of technological development.

12. _____ _____ _____ refers to the level of reproduction that maintains population at a steady state.

13. The concentration of humanity into cities refers to _____.

14. A _____ is a large city that socially and economically dominates an urban area.

15. The _____ are urban areas beyond the political boundaries of a city.

16. A _____ is a vast urban region containing a number of cities and their surrounding suburbs.

17. _____ is a type of social organization by which people are closely tied by kinship and tradition.

18. _____ is a type of social organization by which people come together only on the basis of self-interest.

19. _____ _____ is the study of the link between the physical and social dimensions of cities.

20. _____ is the study of the interaction of living organisms and the natural environment.

21. The _____ _____ refers to the earth's surface and atmosphere, including living organisms, air, water, soil, and other resources necessary to sustain life.

22. An _____ is a system composed of the interaction of all living organisms and their natural environment.

23. _____ _____ refers to profound and long-term harm to the natural environment caused by humanity's focus on short-term material affluence.

24. _____ _____ are regions of dense forestation, most of which circle the globe close to the equator.

25. _____ _____ refers to a rise in the earth's average temperature caused by an increasing concentration of carbon dioxide and other gases in the atmosphere.

26. _____ _____ refers to the pattern by which environmental hazards are greatest for poor people, especially minorities.

27. An _____ _____ _____ is a way of life that meets the needs of the present generation without threatening the environmental legacy of future generations.

PART IV: IMPORTANT RESEARCHERS

In the space provided below each of the following researchers, write two or three sentences to help you remember his or her respective contributions to the field of sociology.

Ferdinand Tönnies

Emile Durkheim

Robert Park

Louis Wirth

Georg Simmel

PART V: STUDY QUESTIONS

True-False

1.   T   F   *Malthusian theory* predicted that while population would increase in a *geometric progression*, food supplies would increase only by an *arithmetic progression*.

2.   T   F   According to *demographic transition theory*, population patterns are linked to a society's level of technological development.

3.   T   F   In the mid-eighteenth century, the *Industrial Revolution* triggered a *second urban revolution*.

4.   T   F   Most of the ten *largest cities* in the U.S. today (by population) are in the *Sunbelt*.

5.   T   F   The cultural values of material comfort, progress, and science form the foundation for the *logic of growth* thesis.

6.   T   F   The United States is being characterized in the text as a *disposable society*.

7.   T   F   Households around the world account for more *water use* than does industry.

8.   T   F   The *greenhouse effect* is the result of too little carbon dioxide in the atmosphere.

Multiple Choice

1.   How many people are added to the planet *each year*?

    (a)   5 million
    (b)   23 million
    (c)   51 million
    (d)   73 million

2.   The incidence of childbearing in a country's population refers to

    (a)   fertility.
    (b)   fecundity.
    (c)   demography.
    (d)   sex ratio.
    (e)   life expectancy.

3.   The movement of people into and out of a specified territory is

(a)   demographic transition.
(b)   migration.
(c)   fecundity.
(d)   mortality.
(e)   fertility.

4.   The *sex ratio* in the U.S. is

(a)   85.
(b)   100.
(c)   90.
(d)   105.
(e)   96.

5.   *Demographic transition theory* links population patterns to a society's

(a)   religious beliefs and practices.
(b)   technological development.
(c)   natural resources.
(d)   sexual norms.

6.   According to the text, the *second urban revolution* was triggered by

(a)   the fall of Rome.
(b)   the post-World War II baby boom.
(c)   the Industrial Revolution.
(d)   the discovery of the New World.
(e)   the fall of Greece.

7.   The period of *1950 to the present* is described in the text as

(a)   urban decentralization.
(b)   the metropolitan era.
(c)   urban expansion.
(d)   the second urban revolution.

8.   A vast urban region containing a number of cities and their surrounding suburbs is known as a

(a)   metropolis.
(b)   suburb.
(c)   Gemeinschaft.
(d)   megalopolis.

9.   The link between the *physical* and *social* dimensions of cities is known as

       (a)   Gesellschaft.
       (b)   urban ecology.
       (c)   organic solidarity.
       (d)   mechanical solidarity.
       (e)   demography.

10.   _____ is the study of the interaction of living organisms and the natural environment.

       (a)   Environmentalism
       (b)   Sociobiology
       (c)   Ecosystem
       (d)   Ecology

11.   Which of the following is *not* a projection for the next century using the *limits of growth thesis*?

       (a)   a stabilizing, then declining population
       (b)   declining industrial output per capita
       (c)   declining resources
       (d)   increasing, then declining pollution
       (e)   increasing food per capita

12.   Which type of solid waste represents about *one-half* of all household trash in the U.S.?

       (a)   metal products
       (b)   yard waste
       (c)   paper
       (d)   plastic

13.   While industry accounts for 25 percent of water usage globally, individuals account for _____ percent of usage.

       (a)   90
       (b)   65
       (c)   50
       (d)   25
       (e)   10

14.   *Rain forests* cover approximately _____ percent of the earth's land surface.

       (a)   1
       (b)   7
       (c)   2
       (d)   11

15. A way of life that meets the needs of the present generation without threatening the environmental legacy of future generations refers to

    (a)   ecologically sustainable culture.
    (b)   the Green Revolution.
    (c)   environmental racism.
    (d)   the greenhouse effect.

Matching

1. ___   The earth's surface and atmosphere, including living organisms as well as the air, soil, and other resources necessary to sustain life.
2. ___   The study of the interaction of living organisms and the natural environment.
3. ___   The incidence of childbearing in a society's population.
4. ___   1860-1950.
5. ___   Argued that urbanites develop a blasé attitude, selectively tuning out much of what goes on around them.
6. ___   Regions of dense forestation, most of which circle the globe close to the equator.
7. ___   Developed the concepts of mechanical and organic solidarity.
8. ___   The incidence of death in a country's population

a.	natural environment	e.	rain forests
b.	metropolitan era	f.	ecology
c.	fertility	g.	Georg Simmel
d.	mortality	h.	Emile Durkheim

Fill-In

1. _____ is the incidence of childbearing in a society's population.
2. _____ refers to the incidence of death in a country's population.
3. _____ *theory* is the thesis that population patterns are linked to a society's level of technological development.
4. _____ _____ _____ refers to the level of reproduction that maintains population at a steady state.
5. The _____ _____ refers to the earth's surface and atmosphere, including living organisms, air, water, soil, and other resources necessary to sustain life.
6. An _____ is defined as the system composed of the interaction of all living organisms and their natural environment.
7. Core values that underlie cultural patterns in the U.S. include progress, material comfort, and science. Such values form the foundation for the _____ *thesis.*
8. We need to curb *water consumption* by industry, which uses _____ percent of the global total, and by farming, which consumes _____ of the total for irrigation.

Discussion

1.   What are the three basic factors that determine the *size* and *growth rate* of a population? Define each of these concepts.
2.   Identify and describe the five *periods of growth* of U.S. cities.
3.   What are three factors that are causing *urban growth* in poor societies?
4.   Differentiate between the concepts *ecology* and *natural environment*.
5.   What three important ideas are implied by the concept *environmental deficit*?
6.   Briefly describe the pattern of world *population growth* prior to and after the Industrial Revolution.
7.   Critically differentiate between the *logic of growth* and the *limits to growth* views concerning the relationship between human technology and the natural environment.
8.   What is meant by the term *disposable society*? What evidence is being presented to support this view of the U.S.?

PART VI: ANSWERS TO STUDY QUESTIONS

Key Concepts

1.   Demography (p. 418)
2.   Fertility (p. 418)
3.   crude birth rate (p. 418)
4.   Mortality (p. 419)
5.   crude death rate (p. 419)
6.   infant mortality rate (p. 419)
7.   Life expectancy (p. 420)
8.   migration (p. 420)
9.   sex ratio (pp. 421-22)
10.   age-sex pyramid (p. 422)
11.   Demographic transition theory (p. 423)
12.   Zero population growth (p. 424)
13.   urbanization (p. 426)
14.   metropolis (p. 428)
15.   suburbs (p. 428)
16.   megalopolis (p. 429)
17.   Gemeinschaft (p. 430)
18.   Gesellschaft (p. 430)
19.   Urban ecology (p. 432)
20.   Ecology (p. 434)
21.   natural environment (p. 434)
22.   ecosystem (p. 434)
23.   Environmental deficit (p. 435)
24.   Rain forests (p. 440)
25.   Global warming (p. 441)
26.   Environmental racism (p. 442)
27.   ecologically sustainable culture (p. 444)

1.	T	(p. 423)	5.	T	(p. 436)
2.	T	(p. 423)	6.	T	(p. 437)
3.	T	(p. 427)	7.	F	(pp. 438-439)
4.	T	(p. 429)	8.	F	(p. 441)

Multiple Choice

1.	d	(p. 418)	9.	b	(p. 432)
2.	a	(p. 418)	10.	d	(p. 434)
3.	b	(p. 420)	11.	e	(p. 436)
4.	e	(p. 422)	12.	c	(p. 437)
5.	b	(p. 423)	13.	e	(pp. 438-439)
6.	c	(p. 427)	14.	b	(p. 441)
7.	a	(p. 428)	15.	a	(p. 444)
8.	d	(p. 429)			

Matching

1.	a	(p. 434)	5.	g	(p. 431)
2.	f	(p. 434)	6.	e	(p. 440)
3.	c	(p. 418)	7.	h	(pp. 430-431)
4.	b	(p. 428)	8.	d	(p. 419)

Fill-In

1. Fertility (p. 418)
2. Mortality (p. 419)
3. Demographic transition (p. 423)
4. Zero population growth (p. 424)
5. natural environment (p. 434)
6. ecosystem (p. 434)
7. logic of growth (p. 436)
8. 25, two-thirds (pp. 438-439)

PART VII: IN FOCUS—IMPORTANT ISSUES

- Demography: The Study of Population

   Define each of the following factors that affect *population size:*

   fertility

   crude birth rate

fecundity

mortality

crude death rate

infant mortality rate

migration

immigration

emigration

- History and Theory of Population growth

    Briefly describe the components of each of the following theories of population growth:

        Malthusian theory

        Demographic transition theory

- Urbanization: The Growth of Cities

    Identify and describe the three *urban revolutions*.

    Describe each of the following periods in the *growth of cities* in the United States:

        colonial settlement

        urban expansion

        the metropolitan era

        urban decentralization

- Urbanization as a Way of Life

    How did each of the following theorists characterize cities and the process of *urbanization*?

        Ferdinand Tönnies

        Emile Durkheim

        Georg Simmel

        The Chicago School

            Robert Park

            Louis Wirth

- Urbanization in Poor Societies

    Briefly describe the *third urban revolution*.

- Environment and Society

    Differentiate between each of the following views concerning environmental issues.

        the logic of growth

        the limits to growth

    What are two important points being made in the text concerning each of the following?

        solid waste

        water

        air

- Looking Ahead: Toward a Sustainable World

What are the three recommendations being made for establishing an *ecologically sustainable culture*?

<table>
<tr><td>Chapter</td><td rowspan="2"></td></tr>
</table>

Chapter	Social Change:
16	Modern and Postmodern Societies

Social Change: Modern and Postmodern Societies

Chapter 16

PART I: CHAPTER OUTLINE

I.   What is Social Change?

II.   Causes of Social Change
- A.   Culture and Change
- B.   Conflict and Change
- C.   Ideas and Change
- D.   Demographic Change
- E.   Social Movements and Change
  - 1.   Types of Social Movements
  - 2.   Explaining Social Movements
  - 3.   Stages in Social Movements

III.   Modernity
- A.   Ferdinand Tönnies: The Loss of Community
- B.   Emile Durkheim: The Division of Labor
- C.   Max Weber: Rationalization
- D.   Karl Marx: Capitalism

IV.   Structural-Functional Theory: Modernity as Mass Society
- A.   The Mass Scale of Modern Life
- B.   The Ever-Expanding State

V.   Social-Conflict Theory: Modernity as Class Society
- A.   Capitalism
- B.   Persistent Inequality

VI.   Modernity and the Individual
- A.   Mass Society: Problems of Identity
- B.   Class Society: Problems of Powerlessness

VII.   Modernity and Progress
- A.   Modernity: Global Variation

VIII.   Postmodernity

IX.   Looking Ahead: Modernization and Our Global Future

X.   Summary

XI.   Key Concepts

XII.   Critical-Thinking Questions

XIII.   Applications and Exercises

XIV.   Sites to See

XV.   Investigate with Research Navigator

PART II: LEARNING OBJECTIVES

- To identify and describe the four general characteristics of social change.
- To identify and illustrate the different sources of social change.
- To be able to discuss the perspectives on social change as offered by Ferdinand Tönnies, Emile Durkheim, Max Weber, and Karl Marx.
- To identify and describe the general characteristics of modernization.
- To identify the key ideas of two major interpretations of modern society: mass society and class society.
- To be able to discuss the ideas of postmodernist thinkers and critically consider their relevance for our society.

PART III: KEY CONCEPTS

1. _____ _____ refers to the transformation of culture and social institutions over time.
2. Organized activity that encourages or discourages social change is called a _____ _____.
3. _____ _____ is a perceived disadvantage arising from a specific comparison.
4. _____ refers to social patterns resulting from industrialization.
5. The process of social change begun by industrialization is known as _____.
6. _____ ____ _____ refers to specialized economic activity.
7. _____ is Durkheim's term for a condition in which society provides little moral guidance to individuals.
8. A _____ _____ is a society in which industry and bureaucracy have eroded traditional social ties.
9. A _____ _____ is a capitalist society with pronounced social stratification.
10. _____ _____ refers to personality patterns common to members of a particular society.
11. _____-_____ refers to a rigid conformity to time honored ways of living.
12. _____-_____ refers to a receptiveness to the latest trends and fashions, often expressed by imitating others.
13. _____ refers to social patterns characteristic of postindustrial societies.

PART IV: IMPORTANT RESEARCHERS

In the space provided below each of the following researchers, write two or three sentences to help you remember his or her respective contributions to the field of sociology.

Karl Marx   Max Weber

Emile Durkheim   Ferdinand Tönnies

Peter Berger

168

PART V: STUDY QUESTIONS

True-False

1. T   F   Sociologist Peter Berger suggests that an important characteristic of modernization is the expression of personal choice.
2. T   F   According to our author, Emile Durkheim's view of modernity is both less complex and less positive than that of Ferdinand Tönnies.
3. T   F   Compared to Emile Durkheim, Max Weber was more critical of modern society, believing that the rationalization of bureaucracies would cause people to become alienated.
4. T   F   A *mass society* is one in which industry and bureaucracy have enhanced social ties.
5. T   F   *Class-society theory* maintains that persistent social inequality undermines modern society's promise of individual freedom.
6. T   F   According to David Reisman, a type of social character he labels *tradition-directedness* represents rapidly changing industrial societies.
7. T   F   *Postmodernity* refers to the recent trend in industrialized societies of a return to traditional values and practices.
8. T   F   In effect, *dependency theory* asserts that rich nations achieved their modernization at the expense of poor ones, which provided them with valuable natural resources and human labor.

Multiple Choice

1. The transformation of culture and social institutions over time refers to

   (a) social statics.
   (b) social change.
   (c) cultural lag.
   (d) modernity.

2. _____ is the process of social change begun by industrialization.

   (a) Postmodernity
   (b) Anomie
   (c) Mass society
   (d) Modernization

3. He developed the theory of *Gemeinschaft* and *Gesellschaft*, arguing that the Industrial Revolution weakened the social fabric of family and tradition by introducing a business-like emphasis on facts, efficiency, and money.

   (a) Karl Marx
   (b) Max Weber
   (c) Emile Durkheim
   (d) Ferdinand Tönnies

4   For *Emile Durkheim*, modernization is defined by the increasing _____ of a society.

(a)   mechanical solidarity
(b)   alienation
(c)   division of labor
(d)   conspicuous consumption

5.   In contrast to Ferdinand Tönnies, who saw industrialization as amounting to a loss of solidarity, _____ viewed modernization not as a loss of community but as a change from community based on bonds of likeness to community based on economic interdependence.

(a)   Emile Durkheim
(b)   Karl Marx
(c)   Max Weber
(d)   Peter Berger

6.   For *Max Weber*, modernity means replacing a traditional world view with a _____ way of thinking.

(a)   alienated
(b)   marginal
(c)   mechanical
(d)   organic
(e)   rational

7.   *Karl Marx's* theory underestimated the dominance of _____ in modern society.

(a)   inequality
(b)   alienation
(c)   power
(d)   bureaucracy
(e)   false consciousness

8.   _____ *theory* focuses on the expanding scale of social life and the rise of the state in the study of modernization.

(a)   Dependency
(b)   Modernization
(c)   Social class
(d)   Rationalization
(e)   Mass-society

9. _____ *theory* views the process of modernization as being linked to the rise of capitalism, and sees its effects as involving the persistence of social inequality.

(a) Mass-society
(b) Class-society
(c) Modernity
(d) Cultural lag

10. Which social scientist described *modernization* in terms of its effects on *social character*?

(a) Peter Berger
(b) William Ogburn
(c) David Reisman
(d) Herbert Marcuse
(e) David Klein

11. _____ refers to personality patterns common to members of a particular society.

(a) Mass society
(b) Class society
(c) Traditionalism
(d) Social character
(e) Autonomy

12. _____ *theory* argues that persistent social inequality undermines modern society's promise of individual freedom.

(a) Mass-society
(b) Modernization
(c) Traditional-rational
(d) Mechanical
(e) Class-society

13. _____ suggested that we be critical of *Max Weber's* view that modern society is rational because technological advances rarely empower people; instead, we should focus on the issue of how technology tends to reduce people's control over their own lives.

(a) Emile Durkheim
(b) Herbert Spencer
(c) David Reisman
(d) Herbert Marcuse
(e) Ferdinand Tönnies

14. According to public opinion polls, in which of the following modern societies does the largest percentage of the population believe that *scientific advances* are helping society?

    (a)   Great Britain
    (b)   Japan
    (c)   the United States
    (d)   Canada
    (e)   Mexico

15. The bright light of "progress" is fading; science no longer holds the answers; cultural debates are intensifying; in important respects, modernity has failed; and social institutions are changing--are all themes running through _____ *thinking*.

    (a)   class-society
    (b)   postmodern
    (c)   mass-society
    (d)   social movements

Matching

1. ____ The transformation of culture and social institutions over time.
2. ____ Social patterns resulting from industrialization.
3. ____ Developed the concepts of mechanical and organic solidarity.
4. ____ Argued that modern society was dominated by rationality.
5. ____ Understood modern society as being synonymous with capitalism.
6. ____ A society in which industry and bureaucracy have eroded traditional social ties.
7. ____ A capitalist society with pronounced social stratification.
8. ____ Personality patterns common to members of a particular society.

    a.   mass society   e.   modernity
    b.   social change   f.   social character
    c.   Max Weber   g.   Emile Durkheim
    d.   class society   h.   Karl Marx

Fill-In

1. Focusing on culture as a source, *social change* results from three basic processes: _____, _____, and _____.

2. According to Peter Berger, four major characteristics of *modernization* include: the decline of small, _____ communities, the _____ of personal choice, increasing social _____, and future orientation and growing awareness of _____.

3. _____ is a condition in which society provides little moral guidance to individuals.

4. For Max Weber, modernity amounts to the progressive replacement of a traditional world-view with a _____ way of thinking.

5. *Mass-society theory* draws upon the ideas of _____, _____, and _____.
6. A _____ *society* is a society in which industry and expanding bureaucracy have eroded traditional social ties.
7. _____ *society* is a capitalist society with pronounced social stratification.
8. Five themes have emerged as part of *postmodern thinking*. These include that, in important respects, _____ has failed; the bright promise of "_____" is fading; _____ no longer holds the answers; cultural debates are _____; and social institutions are _____.

Discussion

1. What are four characteristics of *social change*? Further, five general domains that are involved in *causing* social change are identified and discussed in the text. List these and provide an example for each.
2. Differentiate among Ferdinand Tönnies's, Emile Durkheim's, Max Weber's, and Karl Marx's perspective on modernization.
3. What factors of *modernization* do theorists operating from the *mass-society* theory focus on?
4. What are the two types of *social character* identified by David Reisman? Define each of these.
5. What are the arguments being made by *postmodernists* concerning social change in modern society? What do critics of this view say?
6. Four general types of *social movements* are discussed in the text. Identify, define, and illustrate each of these.
7. Four explanations of *social movements* are discussed in the text. Identify and describe each of these.
8. Peter Berger has identified four major characteristics of modernization. What are these? Provide an illustration for each of these.

PART VI: ANSWERS TO STUDY QUESTIONS

Key Concepts

1. Social change (p. 451)
2. social movement (p. 453)
3. Relative deprivation (p. 454)
4. Modernity (p. 455)
5. modernization (p. 455)
6. Division of labor (p. 457)
7. Anomie (p. 458)
8. mass society (p. 459)
9. class society (p. 461)
10. Social character (p. 463)
11. Tradition-directness (p. 463)
12. Other-directness (p. 464)
13. Postmodernity (p. 467)

True-False

1.	T	(p. 456)	5.	T	(p. 461)
2.	F	(p. 458)	6.	F	(p. 463)
3.	T	(p. 459)	7.	T	(pp. 467-468)
4.	T	(p. 459)	8.	T	(p. 470)

Multiple Choice

1.	b	(p. 451)	9.	b	(pp. 461-462)
2.	d	(p. 455)	10.	c	(p. 463)
3.	d	(pp. 456-457)	11.	d	(p. 463)
4.	c	(pp. 457-458)	12.	e	(pp. 464-465)
5.	a	(p. 458)	13.	d	(p. 465)
6.	e	(pp. 458-459)	14.	c	(p. 465)
7.	d	(p. 459)	15.	b	(p. 468)
8.	e	(pp. 459-460)			

Matching

1.	b	(p. 451)	5.	h	(p. 459)
2.	e	(p. 455)	6.	a	(p. 459)
3.	g	(pp. 457-458)	7.	d	(p. 461)
4.	c	(pp. 458-459)	8.	f	(p. 463)

Fill-In

1. invention, discovery, diffusion (p. 452)
2. traditional, expansion, diversity, time (pp. 455-456)
3. Anomie (p. 458)
4. rational (p. 458)
5. Tönnies, Durkheim, Weber (p. 459)
6. mass (p. 459)
7. Class (p. 461)
8. modernity, progress, science, intensifying, changing (pp. 468-469)

PART VII: IN FOCUS—IMPORTANT ISSUES

• What is Social Change?

   What are the four major characteristics of the process of *social change*?

- Causes of Social Change

    Provide an illustration for each of the following *causes of social change.*

        culture and change

        conflict and change

        ideas and change

        demographic change

- Modernity

    What are the four major characteristics of *modernization*?

    Briefly summarize the view of modernity as expressed by each of the following theorists:

        Ferdinand Tönnies

        Emile Durkheim

        Max Weber

        Karl Marx

- Theoretical Analysis of Modernity

    According to structural-functionalists, what are the essential characteristics of *mass society*?

According to conflict theorists, what are the essential characteristics of *class society*?

- Postmodernity

    What are the five themes shared by *postmodern* thinkers?

- Looking Ahead: Modernization and Our Global Future

    How do *modernization theory* and *dependency theory* shed light on issues raised in this chapter concerning modernization?